Don't Abandon Your Baby!

True Life Stories of Babies That Were Almost Abandoned

Adventures in the world of hidden pregnancies:
rescuing frightened girls and women while
saving their babies from abandonment or even death.

By Debbe Magnusen

Don't Abandon Your Baby!

Published by DeDay Publishing

For information or to contact Debbe write to:
Project Cuddle, Inc.
2973 Harbor Blvd., #326
Costa Mesa, CA 92626-3989

Cover Design: Elizabeth W. Richards and Rick Rainey

Library of Congress Card Number
ISBN   0-9664196-1-8

1. Title   2. Family/Childcare   3. Child Abuse   4. Baby
Abandonment   5. Adoption   6. Biography
7. Alternative life-style   8. Pregnancy   9. Self Help

Printed by: Golden Belt Printing, Inc.
PO Box 997
Great Bend, KS 67530

NOTE: Some of the stories in this book have had names, locations, dates and identifying characteristics changed in order to protect the privacy and safety of the people involved.

Foreward

I'm having a tea party to introduce my friends to a woman named Debbe Magnusen. She has started an organization called Project Cuddle. They rescue abandoned babies. I knew immediately that I had to go to my friend's get-together on that Sunday afternoon. I didn't know that it would be the beginning of this incredible journey filled with tears, laughter, fear and hope.

Debbe is an extraordinary woman, filled with huge levels of compassion, and patience, along with a deep desire to right the sometimes insurmountable wrongs of this issue known as baby abandonment. With her courage, her strength, and her determination to find a home for every little one who graces this earth, she has been an inspiration not only to me, but also to the thousands of women, men and children with whom she has come in contact.

When I read her first book **It's Never Dull!!**, I was overcome with thoughts and feelings that I had never felt before when faced with this troubling issue. I found myself not as quick to judge. Before, it was so easy to ask myself, "How could anyone just leave their baby in a dumpster? Or a trash can?" or "Well, those girls must all be on drugs." Those attitudes were quickly changed as each story had its own unique compilation of similar feelings that these young and not so young women faced—confusion, shame, isolation, fear, and hopelessness. Debbe has been a beacon of light for these women. Sometimes the only ray of hope in a situation rampant with despair.

As I have heard many stories from Debbe, and have seen countless photos of the little ones who are born into this world while their mothers are no longer worried about their outcome, or the tragedy that could have come about if Debbe was not there, I am filled with hope for the future—for women and for babies.

I'm sure you will find the upcoming stories incredibly moving in many different ways. And perhaps, as in my case, you will be forever inspired with the knowledge that one person can make a huge difference.

Gloria Reuben

Dedication

This book is dedicated to all the girls, young and old, who bravely put their trust in Project Cuddle when they felt frightened and had no where to turn. Also for being willing to give their babies a chance at life when they could have easily chosen abandonment or death. To my wonderful husband Dave, my children Brian, Lani, Bejay, Beth, Emily, Tyler and Jonathon. To my son Brian's wife Talea, the mother of my first grandchild, little Abigail. You have all shared so much by having pregnant girls in our home, sharing food, beds, time and space. For all of your patience when I was answering a crisis call in the midst of a road trip, or missing a performance because I was coaching in the delivery of a baby. Many babies are safe today because of your unselfish attitudes.

Dave, you have stood by me for over 25 years and for that, you deserve more than words can say. To my awesome staff, I thank you for hanging in there when one day seems to blend in with another.

Debbe Magnusen

Acknowledgements

I need to thank some very special people for helping Project Cuddle get off the ground. Chris and Anne Mancuso of Clear World Communications, thank you just doesn't seem enough. We are forever grateful to you for your kindness and generosity. To my parents, Dick and Scotty Pyle: I know you had your doubts, but I know now that you believe in me and I appreciate that. I love you both very much. Liz Richards, you are so wonderful. You helped me keep writing when I wasn't sure that I could. I thank you for your knowledge and willingness to try and teach me new things while editing.

To my dear friend, Yvette Taylor: I am so glad that you and Miss Cameron are a part of my life. Your cheery voices seem to always revive me when I need a pick-me-up. Thanks for always being there for me. This book wouldn't be possible without the time, care and assistance of the Project Cuddle staff. Angel Waters, you are an awesome Office Manager and a "Partner in Crime." Thank you for helping to get us into the new millennium. Rick and Linda Rainey, thanks for your help with media and marketing. Your talent and expertise are greatly appreciated. Roy and Jackie Myers, thank you for your help in editing this book.

To Ricki Lake and Chris Albert, I thank you so very much for giving us the opportunity to share our message on "The Ricki Lake" show. Hundreds have been helped because of this, and babies are alive, in part because of you and Columbia Tristar Television. To the Project Cuddle Board of Directors, your guidance, direction and dedication have proven to be invaluable. Steven Lazarus, you are a wonderful adoption attorney. You have always been there when girls needed help, and not charged for the endless hours spent. I thank you for having a heart as big as the ocean. Thank you Sheli Hinds for all you have done to promote Project Cuddle. You are a wonderful supporter and friend. Rosa Clark, thanks for being such a great social worker and always being able to make me laugh.

Thanks so much to Gene and Linda Campbell for all your love and passion to help Project Cuddle in its efforts to stop baby abandonment. Crystal Martell, Marjorie Davis, Elizabeth McKibbin, Dee Lacy, Joann Lowy and Tammy French, I want to thank you for all the time and energy you have spent acting as cheerleaders for our cause. To all the phone operators who make the lines so warm and welcoming to each girl or woman who calls, thank you. Thanks to each volunteer across the country who has pitched in at a moment's notice. Without you, we couldn't do all that we do.

To Graham and Vernelle Kerr. I hope you realize how special you both are. Thanks for all your support; I'm so honored that you believe in Project Cuddle and in me. I love you both.

D.M.

Introduction

For over five years, I have been able to work with and experience the thoughts of frightened girls and women who find themselves pregnant and cannot accept it. I call this condition "Pregnexia"—denial of one's pregnancy. Whether it is because they were raped, or in an abusive relationship where the pregnancy could actually have lead to death, something has caused them to become paralyzed with fear. They cannot accept the pregnancy. Sometimes it's a case of incest and others are straight "A" students with such a strong desire to make their parents happy that pregnancy just isn't an option.

I believe that God allows everything to happen for a reason. Sometimes it may take awhile for the reason to be revealed to us. I went through my second, planned pregnancy in 1978 and actually experienced so many of the symptoms of "Pregnexia". I contracted mononucleosis and bronchial pneumonia with a heart rate of 160 while sitting still. (A normal heart rate is between 70 to 80 beats a minute.) I was told that I was a walking time bomb and that both the baby and I could die at any time during the pregnancy. Needless to say, I didn't look at this pregnancy as I did with the first, I did not rub my belly, and I still slept on my stomach until the day I delivered. I could not accept that there was a baby inside me. Because if I did and lost the baby, I felt it would be too much for me to handle. I can honestly say that I didn't feel the baby kick or move. I use to think "it" must be dead. No worries, no real feelings at all. Here's how unattached I was. I woke up on the morning the baby was due and had some pains. I never even thought that I was having contractions. I actually told myself, "No more baked beans." I just figured it was a case of bad gas. After discovering that my bloody show had presented itself, I realized that this gas I had been having every two minutes was actually labor. In my mind I did not accept that I was pregnant and therefore I could not accept that I was in labor. This experience allows me to understand the girls and women with whom I now work.

My hope is that in the pages that follow you will see through my eyes and hopefully we can all learn how to better prevent baby abandonment, infanticide and neonaticide. I am so thankful for the chance to learn from each of these girls and women whom I have met. They have taught me so much. I hope that you too will learn from their experiences. Hopefully we can learn enough from their experiences so that we can find ways to spread the word about Project Cuddle's 24-hour toll-free crisis hot-line (1-888-628-3353) and prevent baby abandonment, infanticide and neonaticide. This would truly be a dream come true.

Table of Contents

Chapter One

Somebody's Got a Secret

Introduction

Little did I know that after fostering over 34 drug-exposed babies, my life would take another turn and I would be starting my own crisis line that would save babies' lives. What I expected is not what happened. What I hoped for became even more exciting and awesome than I could ever have expected. The following chapter, "Somebody's Got a Secret", shares a portion taken from my first book, **It's Never Dull!!** and how I began saving babies from abandonment. I also share stories of young women where I assisted with their secret pregnancy.

My First Rescue

"You better figure something out, or I'm putting it in the park when it's born!" she demanded. The woman on the other end of the line was serious. She went on to tell me that she hated her unborn baby. It was only twelve hours after we opened the crisis line that we got our first call. It wasn't what I had expected at all.

For the past four months we rehearsed the way that the crisis line would be answered and how our procedures would be put into play. This wasn't how it was supposed to go. You see, we actually thought that we would get the calls after the woman had given birth. She was going to tell us where she had left the baby and then we would send the authorities out to pick it up. Well, at least for me, nothing ever goes as planned.

Reality was setting in and I was going to have to act quickly and reprogram everything. To top it all off, the poor frightened woman only spoke Spanish. We found out her name was Teresa. My husband Dave and my friend Pilar went to the local park where the woman had instructed us to meet her. There stood a Hispanic woman in her early twenties. She had a little boy that clung to her side. Dave and Pilar brought her back to our home where I began to learn the horrible details that lead to this very moment.

Teresa brought little Jose into the living room. I knew that she wanted to talk but was uncomfortable with the thought of Jose hearing what she was about to say. Our little two-year old Jonathon was able to help us out by taking little Jose out into the back yard. It was amazing. Neither of them spoke the same language, but they were good buddies within minutes. I had seen how well

15

Teresa cared for Jose and so I couldn't figure out why she would hate *this* baby so much. I was about to learn why.

In October of that past year, Teresa had gone to a party with some friends. They stopped by the neighborhood bar afterwards and that's where she met an "African-American" with whom she danced on that fateful evening. She and her girlfriends loved to pick up guys and dance for hours on end. Yes, she may have been Mexican but she was crazy about America's music from the 70's. As she spoke about the music, her eyes lit up. It was as though she temporarily forgot that she was carrying a baby in her swollen belly. Her face became more serious as she remembered where this great evening of dancing with this man went. He knew all the right moves and she thought he was the best dancer she had ever seen. She spoke of how she had walked out of the bar with this man thinking it was a wonderful evening. He seemed nice enough and she offered to have him come over to her apartment for a drink. Her ex-boyfriend had custody of their son for the weekend, so she was free to just kick back and relax for a change. What ended up happening would change her life forever.

Teresa never reported that she had been raped. She was too embarrassed and ashamed as most girls are. She didn't even know his name and didn't want anyone else to find out. What would happen if her ex-boyfriend found out she had been with a man of a different race? He was very prejudiced and was just looking for a reason to be able to take Jose away from her. He wanted his son to be a real man and was afraid that Teresa would turn him into a "mama's boy."

Around April of 1996, Teresa realized that her body had made some changes. She had been trying to hide it from herself, but now she knew the truth—she was pregnant. That horrible night when she was raped had just come back to haunt her and she had no idea what to do. All she knew was that she would need to take Jose and get out of the immediate area as soon as possible.

No one was to learn of this horrible mistake. Teresa found a room to rent just one town away. She could tell that the family

16

renting her the room was so busy with all their own relatives and daily dramas that they wouldn't even notice her or her growing belly. Teresa thought she had it all figured out. The park was only one block from the house, so she planned that when she was ready to deliver she would be able to slip away into the night over to the gully that ran alongside the park. With no houses or apartments in the area, she would be able to scream and no one would hear her cries or yells of pain. With so many shrubs in the park area she could even deliver in the daytime and still be well hidden from people driving by.

Originally, Teresa planned on dumping her baby in the park without even a second thought. She was going to do what she thought she had to do: whatever it took for her to save the son she already had from being handed over to his abusive father. Teresa would never let that happen.

We didn't have much time to try and fix this situation. Pilar and I spoke with Teresa for hours and as we took her back to the park where we had first met, we still did not know if she was going to be willing to work with us. As I walked out the front door I showed her a wicker laundry basket that was lined with a clean new comforter. I had Pilar explain that if she went into labor in the middle of the night and delivered, she could leave the baby in this basket on my front porch, then ring the doorbell and walk away. We also told her that if she was willing to trust us, we would be happy to help her find a safe, legal solution so she didn't have to put it in a trash can, park or dumpster. We didn't want Teresa to go to jail and our best leverage was to tell her that we didn't want little Jose to end up in foster care or back with her violent ex-boyfriend. Now, all we could do was to pray and wait. Teresa was going to have to do some real soul-searching and there was no time to waste.

If we could work through this crisis, we would have turned Project Cuddle into something that was even more incredible than I had ever imagined. We were not only saving a baby from abandonment but also saving the mother from breaking the law. When this was over, she would be able to walk away with her older son, her head held high, and her newborn child would have a chance at life.

The following morning we got the call we had been hoping for. Teresa sounded much happier than when we had last spoken. She said that she had thought everything over, and wanted to give the baby a chance. She asked us to pick her up and she would help us find a solution that she could live with.

Pilar and I drove up towards the park but, this time we passed it by. Teresa had actually given us her address, which I felt very good about. She was actually opening up to us. We loaded her things into the trunk of the car and headed for our place.

I was able to locate an attorney who specialized in adoptions. She came right over and we began to talk through the steps that would need to be taken. The attorney was able to help us find an obstetrician as well as a hospital to care for Teresa and the new baby. People do not realize that most obstetricians will not care for a woman who has had no prenatal care. They are afraid of the liability.

I had to excuse myself to the dining room because a volunteer had shown up at my door. Her name was Sara. I didn't want her to see Teresa because I knew that Teresa was very fearful of everything at this time. I greeted Sara at the door. She was a sweet little woman in her early thirties. She was a fairly new volunteer with a very strong desire to help prevent baby abandonment. For the past four years she and her husband Billy had tried having an *in vitro* baby. They had tried everything and eventually became pregnant through *in vitro*. She had actually become pregnant about a year into the treatments, but miscarried in her fourth month. This had been emotionally devastating to both Sara and Billy. Sara had originally seen us on a local news segment. She so desperately wanted a child to love and hold in her arms and was frustrated that there were women dumping babies out as though they were yesterday's trash. She was now on a mission. She was going to stop by and pick up her second stack of bumper stickers. Sara worked at a local college and was going to do everything in her power to try and spread the word to girls who needed help.

I apologized for not being able to let her in the other room and

18

at the same time was also excited to share the fact that we had actually gotten our first crisis case. I couldn't divulge any of the details of the situation, but I did let her know that we were going to need to find a family that was interested in adopting this baby and could pay for the medical expenses. When Sara heard that she really perked up: "You know, my husband and I would probably be interested. I know it's not up to you, but we would sure appreciate it if you could at least tell her about us."

I told her that I would let the attorney know and that she should write a letter to the birthmother and send along a photo. Sara picked up the stack of bumper stickers and left my home with a smile on her face. Even if it wasn't going to be her baby, there was hope. Hope for her and hope for this baby.

After Sara left, I went back into the living room and I told the attorney about the woman who had just left. I explained what difficulties they had experienced in trying to become parents and what I had recommended she do if she was truly interested in adopting this baby. I received a call back from Sara just as I was finishing up this conversation. She and her husband were serious about the decision to adopt. They were going to stop by with a letter and photo within the hour.

By the end of that evening Teresa had made her decision. She was going to give this baby a chance at life. She was willing to let Sara and Billy adopt the baby as long as she didn't have to be any part of its life. We explained to her that she would need to meet with the adoptive family. Teresa wasn't at all happy about that. She wanted to remain anonymous. We wanted to make it as comfortable as possible for her and so we explained that she just needed to see them for a few minutes. Legally, she needed to meet the family face to face in order for the adoption to progress. Whenever a private adoption occurs, it is to take place by two willing parties that know each other and choose each other. Without that meeting we wouldn't be able to honestly say that they knew each other. We were really running short on time. This baby could arrive at any moment and we had to get Teresa convinced to meet with the family as well as get her to the doctor. My thought was that every pregnant woman craves food, so I figured that if I asked her what kind of food she was craving we might be able to get her comfortable as well as get things done. She perked up when I mentioned food and then got very embarrassed. She told us she loved Chinese food. We were all shocked and all laughed when she told us. It helped in relaxing the atmosphere because she began to join in and laugh with us as well. I told her that we would treat her to lunch after getting her to her doctor's appointment the following day.

Before going to the doctor's appointment we needed to meet with Sara and Billy. Teresa began to get uncomfortable as that time approached. She was so definite about not wanting to have anything to do with them. I reminded her of the Chinese lunch that was awaiting her at the end of this day and I told her that I would have them just walk in and say hello and then walk out if she wanted it that way. Finally she agreed. When Billy and Sara came to the door I greeted them and escorted them into the dining room. Little Jose and Jonathon were busy playing with Legos® under the table while Teresa was nervously sitting next to the attorney. Both Sara and Billy came in and shook hands with the attorney. When they approached Teresa, Sara leaned over and gave her a hug, Billy did the same. I asked Teresa if it was all right for them to stay for a few minutes and she said it would be fine. Her fears began to disappear with the soft loving hugs.

After signing all the proper documents we headed off to the doctor's appointment. Teresa was feeling so much better that she rode with Sara and Billy in their car. We filled out the paper work at the doctor's office and gave him a check to cover the cost of this delivery. I could see that the tension and fears that had surrounded Teresa only a day ago were now disappearing. All her fears of being discovered were only her imaginings. Now that Teresa had faced her "ghosts" she discovered that we could be trusted and could really help her.

The doctor was a sweet little Asian man in his mid-forties with a cute accent. This made it more challenging to translate into Spanish. I didn't want to tell Teresa that the doctor said it could be up to two more weeks before she would deliver, so I told her everything else he had said. I figured that I would tell her later that day about how much longer she could be in this "condition." She was already so mad at this baby that sometimes Pilar would come in crying because of the awful things that Teresa would say. Teresa didn't just not want this baby, but she hated it as well. It was as though this was the baby's fault. Pilar was so hurt and did not understand Teresa's thinking.

Teresa had loosened up so much with Sara and Billy that she had allowed Sara into the room to hear the baby's heart beat. Billy was content just to wait in the waiting room and know that his wife was living the dream of her life. He asked me if it would be all right to give a little gift to Jose. He had struck up quite a friendship while waiting for the exam to be completed. I went in and asked Teresa if she wanted Billy and Sara to leave or if they could join us for Chinese food. With a smile on her face she said that she wanted them to join us. Teresa said there was a little market next door and so we stopped in just long enough for Jose to pick out the perfect little toy truck. As the adults began eating, Jose drove his little yellow '57 Chevy pickup across the dinner table. Teresa loved him so very much and I knew that deep down inside she was a good person, but just not capable of dealing with the situation in front of her.

We had made it through Friday and now that I had told Teresa that it could be two weeks longer, she became very upset. The counselor had met with Teresa, the doctor was lined up and the pre-admit paperwork was in at the hospital. All we could do was wait.

Saturday morning held a few surprises. When I awoke, I was shocked to hear Teresa shouting in Spanish at Pilar. I asked Pilar to translate what the problem was. She told me that if we didn't get the baby out of her belly TODAY, Teresa was threatening to cut it out of herself. She said, "I'm not going to carry this baby any longer. You had better figure something out now!" I could tell by the look on Pilar's face that she knew how serious Teresa was.

As I put a call into the doctor, Pilar decided to try and get Teresa's mind off her problem by taking her and her son to the corner market. It didn't work at all. By the time they got back, Pilar was a nervous wreck. Teresa had been lifting her son up on top of her belly the whole time they were gone with the hope of pushing the baby down. That wasn't the only thing that had happened. Teresa had actually been climbing over a fence in hope that she might move things along.

The doctor returned my call right away and told us to go over to the emergency room and asked them to take a look at Teresa. First they hooked her up to the fetal monitor and at that point they saw no sign of contractions. The only way to guarantee that the baby would be safe to deliver now was to do an ultrasound. Because it was the weekend this could only be done in the hospital. This procedure was going to cost over $1,000. Sara and her husband just did not feel that they could afford that much when they had so many additional and unexpected expenses since the adoption happened so fast. I do not think they realized how very serious and angry Teresa was. It was a real juggling act because we didn't want them to panic, but we didn't want Teresa to injure herself either. All I could do was pray that something would start happening on that fetal monitor. My prayers were answered. Though she was not in labor when we arrived that morning, she was starting to have some contractions. The nurses were very understanding and were glad to see that things were actually starting to happen. Things continued to progress and I was now going to end up being "the coach" for someone who didn't speak any English. Pilar was at my home with all seven of my children, her two, and little Jose.

To my surprise, I learned a couple of new Spanish words that day. I learned the word for push and I figured out on my own what the words "No puedo!" meant. Every time she would have a contraction she would yell this out loud. By the time we were close to her delivery, I had figured out that this meant, "I can't!" Nobody needed to translate that for me. All I could do was nod my head yes and then tell her it was okay.

As the nurse put the call in to the doctor, I asked Teresa if it would be all right if Sara and Billy came in to see her for a minute. I always think it's important for the adoptive family to see what each woman has to go through in order to provide them with such a wonderful gift. They can see how painful this whole process is and at the same time perhaps, help her to lean on them a bit—maybe let the expectant adoptive mother place a washcloth on her forehead. It can be a real bonding time for both. Someday, maybe Teresa's child will learn from her adoptive parents how strong and brave she was.

Teresa was wheeled into the labor room and I held her hand as we entered the sterile delivery room where she would soon deliver her second child. I signaled for Sara and Billy to follow me in. I pointed to the back corner of the room where I thought they should stand. We didn't want Teresa to be any more uncomfortable than she already was. They quietly stood there as the doctor, nurse and I coached Teresa.

Finally, the baby's head was out and as Teresa began to push again, I blurted out, "No one talk about what is going to happen here." I didn't want Teresa to have to hear shouts of joy and the sex of the baby. One more good push and the baby was born. Teresa did not want to see or hear the baby. So as quickly as it was born, I watched the nurse grab it in a towel and head towards the couple in the corner. They were so shocked that they just stood there. I pulled the mask down from my face just long enough to lean towards them and mouth, "It's a girl." They just stood at the back of the room in shock. I now had to mime to them the motion of taking a picture. "Oh!" Sara said as she began to take photos. I leaned over and told Teresa how wonderful she was as tears streamed down my face.

I watched as the Banks family left the room. They pulled their masks down as they followed behind the nurse carrying their new daughter. You could see the joy on both of their faces. Tears streamed down Sara's cheeks as she looked at her new little miracle.

I stayed with Teresa as they began to clean her up. I really wanted to take a peek in the nursery, but knew that right now my place was with Teresa. It took almost an hour before we were ready to leave the operating room. We had been able to arrange for Jose to sneak in for a peek. As she was wheeled into the hallway, there was her precious son, Jose. She reached out for him and knew that everything would now go back to normal.

I finally got to take a few minutes and go into the nursery. I saw Sara and Billy with their new daughter and broke down. I knew this was to be the beginning of something very special. Sara saw me standing by the nursery door and motioned for me to come on over. We embraced and cried for a few minutes. I still have the photo of that moment that someone took and every time I look at it that wonderful feeling of accomplishment returns. I want to always remember that feeling. It's something that you can never fully express in writing, and it's awesome!

✧✧ UPDATE ✧✧

Teresa has moved on with her life; she and Jose have relocated. She still goes dancing on weekends, but is much more careful. She likes her work and is learning English.

The Banks are a true family. They adore their daughter but will never forget that roller-coaster week back in 1996.

The Bathtub Baby

May 1997

"I'm really not feeling very good," Carrie told me as we talked on the phone. All I knew about this frightened 18-year old was that she lived somewhere in Houston, Texas, and no one there knew that she was pregnant. She lived with her mother and even though she assumed she only had about one month to go before she would deliver, she had been able to hide it from her mother and friends. She had cut down on her eating and was always wearing baggy clothes or carrying something in front of her belly.

Carrie and I had spoken on the phone almost every day for the past week. I finally convinced her to go with one of our volunteers for prenatal care. The clinic was all booked up, so she wasn't going to be able to get in for another week, but we assumed we had some time. WRONG!!!

This particular time that I spoke with Carrie, I realized that she would make a grunting sound about every two minutes or so. She told me that she was sick with the flu, but as we spoke I began to realized that this wasn't the flu we were dealing with, but labor pains every two minutes. I began timing these sounds as we kept our conversation going. I was afraid that if I said the wrong thing she would hang up and I wouldn't be able to save this baby or Carrie.

I told Carrie, "Sweetheart, you're not sick with the flu, you're in labor." She told me this wasn't possible. After all, she had just begun to accept the fact that she was pregnant, but this was way too

25

soon for her to deliver, so she thought. I told her that she should call 9-1-1. She wouldn't! I knew that we didn't have much time to figure something out.

Finally, I realized what to do. I would send Kristi, a local volunteer over to Carrie's place. Carrie would soon get a phone call from Kristi and need to give her the address where she lived. This was our only hope. It took me a few minutes, but I was able to convince Carrie to let Kristi have her address. I explained to Carrie that Kristi would come over with some soup and soda and check on her while she was "sick" with the flu. Kristi was going to be my eyes. Once she was on the scene we would truly be able to get Carrie the help she needed.

It seemed as though it took hours for Kristi to get there and call me. Finally, the call came in, "Debbe, it's Kristi. We're on the way to the hospital. I'm following the ambulance!" Kristi began to tell me what had transpired since I last spoke with Carrie. When Kristi had arrived at the apartment, she knocked on the door. She heard a voice inside tell her to come on in. She opened the door to the apartment and said, "Hi Carrie, it's Kristi."

Kristi kept calm as she asked, "Well, how about getting you out of that tub and into an outfit. We'll get you to see a doctor." Carrie agreed to do just that. Kristi set down the chicken soup on the bathroom counter and went behind the old, claw foot tub; she placed her arms under Carrie's arms and began to help get her to a standing position. "Oh my God!" Carrie blurted. "It didn't hurt like this the last time!" She caught herself as she realized the words that had come out of her mouth and the fact that someone had heard her words as well. Though no one had ever known that she was now pregnant, we now knew that this wasn't her first child. No one will probably ever know what happened to that first baby, but at least this time they would.

Kristi had tried desperately to convince Carrie to call 9-1-1. This was not going to happen as long as Carrie was alert. After getting a denim dress over Carrie's head, she was able to convince her to head towards the front door. Suddenly, Carrie yelled, "Oh my God, it's here!" "No," Kristi calmly stated. "We need to get you to the hospital." "No!" Carrie yelled, "It's here!" She lifted her dress in order to convince Kristi that this wasn't a joke.

Kristi looked down at the space between Carrie's legs and there, peeking out was the head of a beautiful baby. Kristi quickly knelt down on the ground in front of Carrie and caught the newborn baby as it made its shocking entry into the world. Kristi took the sweatshirt from around her waist and gently wrapped it around the newborn baby. Tears rolled down her face as she realized what had just happened. She located the phone on the end table and quickly dialed 9-1-1. Carrie was pretty out of it by now and didn't even realize what Kristi was doing.

Once the paramedics stabilized Carrie and the baby, the baby was placed on Carrie's lap in a sterile chuck's pad. Carrie didn't want anything to do with the baby and, in her mind, it wasn't going to be hers. Kristi saw how uncomfortable Carrie was with the baby being placed in her arms. Kristi whispered into Carrie's ear, "It's their policy honey. You need to hold him until you get to the hospital. I'll meet you there and hold him after he's stable." They were placed in the ambulance. Carrie had asked to speak with families wanting to adopt this child.

What a relief it was to hear Kristi on her cell phone as she followed behind the ambulance. "I just caught the baby, and am on my way to the hospital to help out. It's a boy!" she proclaimed. Once I heard that the paramedics started an IV on Carrie, and both she and the baby were doing fine, I was able to relax a bit.

✧✧ UPDATE ✧✧

It has been over two years since this miraculous event took place. Carrie ended up telling her mother everything with the help of Kristi. It was a major shock for this mother since she never knew her daughter was ever pregnant. Because Carrie's mother was willing to accept this baby into the family, Carrie began to bond with the child whom she named Dustin. She now lives with her mother and is raising her son. She is continuing to finish school to get a college degree. Carrie shared with me that she just never wanted to let her mother down. She will be the first in her family to finish college and was so afraid that her mother would be disappointed in her. Now Carrie realizes that her fears were unfounded. Carrie hopes to someday speak out to others who may be in this same position. "I don't ever want anyone else to go through what I did. I made a mistake, but thank God it turned out all right," Carrie says.

My Basketball Babe

Project Cuddle just finished taping the show "EXTRA," and calls were pouring in left and right. There was one call though that really touched me. On the other end of the line was a very frightened young lady by the name of Alexa. Alexa was an 18-year-old student at the University of Oklahoma and was on a full scholarship for basketball. She was in tears because she was now beginning to accept the fact that she was pregnant and felt very vulnerable because we knew her secret.

When Alexa saw the show, she immediately called the Project Cuddle crisis hot line for help. It took me almost five minutes to calm her down. She wouldn't give us a phone number, but did allow me to have her pager number. Though it made it more difficult, I was just happy to have some link to her. She shared with me how she had been raped many months earlier and now she was about 7 ½ months pregnant. One of the other girls on her team had just told the coach she was pregnant and that girl was promptly kicked off the team and sent home. This left Alexa nervous and apprehensive.

Though these challenges seemed great, they were not my main concern. I found out that Alexa had a pacemaker put in just a little over a year prior to this. My first thought is, we have to move quickly to try and get her to see a doctor. She refused to go because she was afraid that someone from the school or her small town would see her going into the obstetrician's office.

Because Alexa was so paranoid about losing her scholarship we had to first deal with her school issues. It took about four or five long phone calls but we finally convinced her to speak with her coach. Along with trying to advise Alexa we went over the key points to address and once she explained everything to him, he told her everything would be fine. She would have to take time out from playing basketball until after the baby was born, but she would still be able to keep her scholarship.

Now, Project Cuddle began working on getting her medical care and a place to stay until she delivered. No one was to know that she was carrying a child.

November 2, 1997

I took my kids to John Wayne Airport to pick up Alexa. She felt that she would be better off far away from friends and family. She knew that we would keep her secret safe and wanted to be near her throughout the rest of the pregnancy. Emily, now eight, held up a sign that was drawn with a tube of lipstick I had found in the van. It said, "Welcome Alexa!" It seemed as though every passenger had deplaned and perhaps Alexa had backed out. My heart sank until I saw one more passenger there at the end of the ramp. She was a beautiful, six-foot tall girl with long auburn hair that accentuated her green eyes. Our eyes met and I knew instantly that this had to be our Alexa. I could tell that she was very shy, as she smiled and then lowered her head a bit towards the ground. I approached her and asked, "Alexa?" She nodded yes. I went towards her and gave her a big hug. The ice was broken and she immediately loosened up. We headed towards home where I would introduce her to "the gang," better known as my family. I think I was more nervous than I had previously been because I knew that her pacemaker could be an issue. She looked really good and healthy, and she barely showed. I scheduled a doctor's appointment right away. I would feel a lot better once I knew Alexa and the baby were in good health.

The following morning I took Alexa to the doctor. The doctor verified that she was in very good shape, but wanted an ultrasound to see just how far along the baby was. Alexa was going to begin speaking with families that she thought might be good to consider for adopting her baby. Alexa did not feel any connection to her baby and did not want to keep it.

November 5, 1997

Alexa met with several families but she did not feel comfortable with any of them. I was happy to see that she was getting more involved in thinking about the life she was carrying and was truly looking out for it's best interest. Still, she seemed to think that she had a lot more time than she really did before the baby was to be born.

Alexa was getting ready to go out for the day. She stepped into the shower and slipped. I heard the shower door rattle and then the thud as she hit the shower floor. I knew immediately what had happened. I ran to the bathroom door. "Are you all right?" I called to her. "No. I hit my stomach. Can you help me?" I sent Dave to get the make-shift key we had hidden for such occasions as when our kids would lock themselves in because they were having a tantrum. Upon his return with the key, I quickly opened the bathroom door and went in to assess the damage. I could see her crumpled body lying in the far right corner through the frosted shower doors. I grabbed the dark green towel and opened the shower door just enough to reach through and give her a chance to cover up a bit. Once she was covered up, I asked her if it was okay to open the door so I could help her. She told me it was okay. She had her one leg up behind her and was holding onto her right side. I told her that she was probably just fine but I thought she should get to the hospital and be seen by a doctor. She was in severe pain and so scared that she agreed.

I had Dave call 9-1-1 as I sat and comforted Alexa. I could only hope and pray that she and the baby would be all right. Within a few minutes the paramedics from Station Five arrived with sirens blaring. Alexa was so embarrassed by all this attention and the fact that she didn't have any clothing on. I tried to help Alexa relax a bit and make her more comfortable. I joked with her about what a great way it was to pick up on some cute firemen. She smiled, but suddenly felt the pain in her belly.

When the paramedics arrived they gently helped Alexa up and began to take her vitals. Once they were sure she was stable we watched as they placed her into the ambulance and then I rode up front so she wouldn't have to be alone.

After nearly an hour in the E.R. we went in to a small area where they performed an ultrasound. The woman adjusted the monitor so that Alexa could see the image of her baby. "I don't think I want to look," she said. When the woman offered to turn it away, Alexa said, "Oh, never mind. I'll be fine. Just leave it." The woman began by placing a cold clear gel on her belly. It seemed to have grown since her arrival the week before. As the image of Alexa's baby became clear on the screen, I saw tears begin to well up in her eyes. I grabbed a tissue from the counter top and handed it to her, saying, "Pretty incredible, isn't it?" She was so choked up that she couldn't say anything, only nod to confirm the amazing sight.

After we were done, the hospital released her to go home, stay off her feet and rest. If she had any complications, she was to return immediately to the hospital. On our ride home, I asked her how she was feeling. After seeing the ultrasound I thought that Alexa had perhaps changed her mind about what to do with regards to the baby. If that was the case I did not want her to be fearful of telling me. It would be better for everyone that she was honest with her feelings as soon as possible.

I sat down and tried to reassure her that we were there for her no matter what her decision. She had finally realized that she was carrying a life within her, and knowing how compassionate a person Alexa was, I doubted she would be able to go through with her original plans. She decided to confront her parents and I sat by her side as she dialed the phone. They learned that she was almost eight months pregnant and that this baby was going to be half Caucasian

32

and half African-American. They lived in an area where this was not acceptable. Her father was going to have to do a lot of adjusting and Alexa was fearful that he wouldn't be able to do this. She wanted to know where everyone stood before she tried to consider going back home.

I sat by her side as she dialed the phone. She told her father everything. Amazingly, he was willing to accept and love both her and her unborn baby. When Alexa asked him what they would do if the KKK caused trouble, he said, "Well, we'll just up and move if we need to." As I looked at Alexa she had a smile on her face and I could tell things were going to be all right.

Within a week, Alexa flew back to Oklahoma and was greeted with open arms by her family. She called me within 15 minutes of landing because she knew I would be worried. She was so precious.

On December 9th, 1997 I received a call on the Project Cuddle crisis hot-line. It was a very familiar voice. "Hey, it's me," she said. "I just delivered my daughter and wanted you to know." Alexa was still in the recovery room after a C-section but knew that I would worry until I heard from her. Both mother and rescue baby #34 were doing just fine.

✧✧ **UPDATE** ✧✧

Alexa is a wonderful mother to Melissa Jean. Though she never went back to the university, she has no regrets. Her family has been very supportive of her and they often take Melissa for weekends. I am delighted to say I receive a call every year on Melissa's birthday. I got a call just the other day from Melissa. She just turned three. With her southern accent she said, "Hey Debbe. I love you." Then she took the phone and hugged it and then kissed it twice according to Alexa. Just hearing this little one and knowing how we had contributed to the outcome for both Melissa, and her mother was incredible. She was now a little person and well on her way to somewhere special.

I asked Alexa what she would have done if Project Cuddle had not been there. To this day, she still doesn't know. Melissa is so beautiful that she recently entered a baby beauty pageant in her state and walked away with first prize. She received a savings bond that will pay for her first two years of college.

Chapter Two

And Baby Makes Two

Introduction

The Project Cuddle staff and I found that over fifty percent of the girls/women we help have at least one other child. A great percentage of them are fearful of being kicked out if they get pregnant again. You see, often the parents are willing to accept one mistake, but threaten that if it ever happens again the daughter would be kicked out as well as the child that she has grown to love.

On the next pages, you will learn about some of these girls and women and what made them so fearful; what they were thinking and why they felt that everything was so hopeless. You'll discover how we were able to help turn "tragedy" into something much different.

I have some wonderful memories from these girls and women. The babies they carried within were just as special to me. I hope that through this chapter, "And Baby Makes Two," you will be able to see at least a portion of what I have seen and continue to see.

Please Pass the Bleach

November 27, 1996

A call came in from a nineteen-year-old in Cincinnati, Ohio. She told me that she already had one child and couldn't risk having her family find out that she was pregnant again. She told me that before finding our program she had come up with three options. The first option was to leave the baby when it was born at her old neighbor's front porch. She had raised a couple of kids, so she figured that she was a nice enough lady and she would probably take good care of it.

The second option was to go into the hospital under an alias when she delivered. When she was feeling better she would just walk out of the hospital and no one would really know who the baby belonged to. She still had second thoughts about this option because she realized that there would be cameras in and around the hospital and they might possibly be able to track her down.

The third and final option was to leave it in the local cemetery. Since only her best friend knew of the pregnancy and was willing to help her in getting rid of the baby, this was probably the plan she was going to use. She was definitely leaning towards this option. That way she wouldn't have to walk by her old neighbor and see it in the front yard and she wouldn't have to worry about seeing her picture on the ten o'clock news.

The girl's name was Sandy. She had been raised in the foster care system and didn't trust anyone but herself. She had already had a little daughter when she was sixteen years old. She loved the little child she named Amanda. Sandy didn't have money for food or diapers. She and her girlfriend would go into the corner market and sneak diapers and formula out under their coats. Sandy thought that most everyone did that.

The biggest worry Sandy had with this pregnancy was the fear that she would lose Amanda if she gave up the new baby. After talking with Sandy, I found out that she was so desperate to get rid of this baby, she had actually tried drinking bleach on numerous occasions.

In order to help Sandy in making a safe decision, we offered to fly her out to stay with us through the rest of her pregnancy. She had nothing keeping her in Ohio and was very anxious to get a second chance at starting her life over in a fresh way.

December 1, 1996

I met this tiny little blonde at the train station. She had Amanda by her side as she stepped down from the car. Our eyes met, and Sandy knew immediately that I was the one she was here to meet. It was so great to know that she was finally here that I couldn't resist giving her a great big hug as she reached me.

It took us only a minute to gather the baggage she had brought. I had Bejay, my nine-year-old with me and he helped carry her bags to the van. We traveled the ten miles home with little Amanda in the backseat singing who-knows-what at the top of her lungs. This girl was definitely going to be a singer.

When we arrived at the house, the four smaller children greeted Sandy and Amanda. Amanda was just a year younger than my son, Jonathon, so they became instant friends. Emily my daughter, being the nurturer of the family, followed Amanda around the house as she pulled, picked and poked at everything that was down at her level. At one point Jonathon came running up and Amanda followed right behind. "Mommy, my index toe got hurted," he announced. Amanda watched as we bandaged his toe and off they both went.

I think the most unique thing I discovered about Sandy was that she was a survivor. She had never had parenting classes, nor had she been truly parented herself. I hoped that we not only would be able to save her baby, but help her discover how to be a good parent to the child she was keeping. We also wanted to give her some direction as far as education or a career for the future.

We sat down at the dinner table as a family that night with our two extra guests. Sandy turned to me and very seriously stated, "Amanda is on a very strict diet." I looked at the two year old that was not very happy being confined in the highchair. I asked Sandy if she had ever had Amanda in a highchair before. I was pretty sure that I already knew the answer to this question, but wanted to make sure. Sure enough, my hunch was right; this was Amanda's first time in the "chair." When I asked Sandy what this special diet was, she said, "She only eats candy and sodas."

I honestly thought she was joking, but I was wrong. She had been feeding her only junk food since Amanda first started to chew. I explained that this wasn't going to continue as long as they were staying in my home. Oh, it wasn't easy. We had major temper tantrums from Amanda. She thought that we would give in to her demands if she screamed loud enough. It took us a good three days and a very hungry little girl before we were able to convince her that a new and improved healthy diet was all she was going to get.

We passed the peas and roast beef for the second dinner and Sandy asked me what those green things were. She had never had a vegetable before. We taught her about green beans, artichokes and I think the funniest was the avocado. She looked very perplexed at it and tried to take a bite out of it. I had to stop her and explain that it had to be peeled before it could be eaten. She was quite impressed with the huge seed inside. I helped her find a jar so she could put the seed in it and watch it grow into a plant.

The next day we got Sandy to the doctor's for her first prenatal visit. Though she appeared to be very tiny, she was already eight months along. She wouldn't look at the ultrasound and didn't want to even know if it was all right. She was just ready to get the baby out of her body. She wanted it out before New Year's. She had heard about a New Year's Eve party that she wanted to go to, but not if she was still pregnant. The technician told her that it would most likely be born after the middle of January. I stopped on the way home and treated her to lunch. She was finally starting to put on a little weight and I knew if I took her somewhere special she would "pig-out," as she would say.

By the time we got home, Sandy seemed to have perked up. I knew from experience that it was still going to be a rough road ahead, but we'd done it before, so we could do it again.

Over the next few days Sandy decided to talk with some families that she would consider for adopting her baby. She didn't really care much about what they were like. She just wanted to find a family and get it over with. New Year's was fast approaching and she was determined to get this baby out in time to celebrate.

The family that Sandy ended up choosing was a very sweet family. Anna was a nurse in the local hospital and her husband Bob was a pharmacist. Anna and Bob had only been able to dream of having a child. Now, it looked like it was going to become a reality. Anna would stop working as soon as the baby came so she could be a full-time mom. This baby was going to have a great family.

December 23, 1996

It was one week before New Year's and Sandy was at her wit's end. She snuck out and went to the local drug store and bought a bottle of castor oil and then drank it. She wanted this baby out NOW! The castor oil didn't work.

Late that afternoon, I got a call from Sandy's roommate. She said Sandy had just moved a large television up the stairs by herself and was not feeling well. This was a girl that was getting desperate. The doctor was called and told that Sandy was having some pains. He suggested that she stay lying down for the next 24 hours and as long as there was no bleeding she should be all right.

40

December 24, 1996

Sandy seemed fine during the night and went back to her apartment in the morning. I got a call about an hour later: "Mom," as she called me, "I'm bleeding." It wasn't what she said as much as how she said it that got me concerned. I asked her why she thought she was bleeding. She then said, "Promise you won't be mad at me." I promised her that I wouldn't and then braced myself for whatever it was that I was about to hear. She said, "I couldn't take it any more. So I got a coat hanger out of the closet." That was all I needed to hear. I knew what the rest of this was going to be. I very calmly told her that she needed to get her bag and I would pick her up in just a minute.

I called the doctor back and told him what Sandy had just done. "I know you don't like to deliver babies early, but I'm afraid this one can't wait." I got Pilar to come over and watch the children and then headed towards Sandy's apartment. By the time I arrived, the doctor told me that I should bring her right to the hospital. We were now walking a fine line between risking infection and endangering the baby.

I called the adoptive family and made them aware of the fact that we were on our way to the hospital. I didn't want to alarm them, so I didn't mention what Sandy had done. I suggested they meet us at the hospital as soon as possible.

Once we arrived at the hospital we were taken immediately back to the labor and delivery area. Fortunately, I had been there so often that they automatically know that the girls need special TLC and are dealing with a different set of issues than the average woman who enters the building.

The doctor started Pitocin in order to get her contractions started. Within a matter of hours, Sandy was ready to deliver. I gowned up and held her hand as she began to endure very strong contractions. Within half an hour I was lifting her head and back forward as she pushed. "Push! Push!" the adoptive family shouted. They looked so excited as they stood back by the door

41

trying to stay out of the way. Sandy had signed papers allowing the adoptive family to be in the delivery room, but up until this point, we had not yet told Sandy that they were there for her. "Hi guys!" she shouted after that contraction passed. "Are we having fun yet?" she asked. "We're here for you sweetie," this soon-to-be mother declared.

At 7:15 p.m. little Meredith Marie made her grand entry into this world as rescue baby #38. Sandy watched as Anna and Bob Watson held their newborn daughter for the first time. Anna had tears running down her face as she realized that this was truly her little girl. She turned toward Sandy and said, "Thank you." Sandy smiled at her and said, "Hey, no problem. I'm glad somebody wants her. I sure don't."

✧✧ UPDATE ✧✧

Sandy is moving forward with her life. Project Cuddle helped Sandy get her GED and then set up childcare while she attended a trade school. Sandy has since married and is doing just fine. She hopes someday she will have another child so that Amanda will have a sibling. We are truly proud of what she has accomplished. The little avocado seed that she placed in water has grown into a tree. It's now growing in the backyard of the home they recently purchased.

One Week 'til "D" Day

August 13, 1997

Project Cuddle appeared on an episode of "48 Hours." After airing, we received some of the most intense crisis calls ever. Three of the girls who called were within a week or two of their assumed delivery dates. None of the girls had had any prenatal care and none thought of telling their families. There was one girl in particular who still makes me smile when I think of her.

To protect her identity, we'll call her Bonnie. Bonnie was from a very small town in Idaho and was pregnant with her second child. Her first child was a little boy by the name of Jason. He was a spunky little fellow with a full head of curly brown hair. He kept Bonnie extremely busy, as he was just about to turn two years old. This pregnancy was a tragedy due to rape. Bonnie hated men. She had been raised by an abusive father and then jilted by the father of her first child as they approached the altar. Now, she had been violated and was carrying a child she wanted nothing to do with. In fact, because of the circumstances of the rape, she didn't even know what the race of the baby was going to be.

After speaking with her on the phone, she decided that she would be willing to have a volunteer accompany her to a neighboring town for at least one prenatal visit. Within 24 hours Bonnie was on her way to her first prenatal appointment. We learned that she was due in the next two weeks and had hidden this from her family and friends. What was truly amazing was that her father was a physician and even he did not notice Bonnie was pregnant.

At first, Bonnie only wanted to talk with single women about adopting her baby. She felt that this would be the safest thing for her baby since she had been so traumatized by men. She decided on one that was out in California where she would be staying with me until she delivered. Luckily we were able to get her a flight for the following day and everything seemed to be going quite well. But it wasn't going to stay that way.

Bonnie's father began to question what she was doing. He wanted to know why Bonnie was going to California and who she was going to be seeing. At this point, Bonnie had to do some quick thinking. She remembered a friend whom she knew out in the Orange County area and so she told him that she was going to see her girlfriend. She wasn't lying. She would visit her friend while out here.

Running this crisis line from my home was not an easy task. Often whatever we were doing was interrupted almost on a daily basis. In order to take a shower I would put the phone by the shower and keep the shower door open so I could see the flashing light since the water would drown out the ringing. The first year we didn't have many volunteers and so we had to stay home the majority of the time. This meant missing birthdays, weddings and even our own anniversary. Often I didn't get but a few hours of solid sleep in a night, but I wouldn't change that for anything. I think Dave suffered the most. I would get a crisis call in the middle of the night and sometimes the conversation could take an hour or so. I'd have to turn the bedroom light on in order to write down information and I wouldn't dare put a girl on hold for fear that she would hang up.

Even though our seven children were all living at home with us, Dave and I felt we should invite Bonnie and Jason to stay with us. I used my credit card to charge two airline tickets. I had no idea how I would pay for them when the bill came, but I knew that I had to get Bonnie out right away. There were three precious lives at stake. We arranged transportation to the nearest airport which was over eight hours away. Bonnie needed to rest before getting on her flight the following morning so I had to call ahead to find a hotel near the airport that would take a credit card over the phone. This wasn't an easy job. It took calls to nine different hotels before I was able to accomplish this. Bonnie and her son Jason were able to rest up before they left beautiful Idaho.

August 16, 1997

The following morning Bonnie and Jason prepared for their two-hour flight. Once the volunteer called to let me know that Bonnie and Jason were safely on board, I was able to relax. My relaxed state didn't last long. I received a call from the woman who had been asked by Bonnie to adopt her baby. She said she needed to come over and talk with me. I couldn't even imagine what she was going to say. The woman arrived within thirty minutes. I figured I would listen to whatever she had to tell me and would still have time to make a sign to display at the airport for Bonnie's arrival in an hour.

As she entered my house, she couldn't help but notice that our son Tyler was atop the refrigerator. When she said "hi" to him, he said, "Hi, I'm a gargoyle. Want anything in the 'fridge?'" She chuckled as she followed me into the living room where a few more of my seven children were playing. It wasn't easy to find a quiet place in this house. After we sat down, she proceeded to tell me why she needed to talk. She had tried three attempts at artificial insemination and none of them had taken. This was her fourth and final attempt and she hadn't even mentioned it because she didn't want to give herself any false hopes. She had just gone to the doctor and found out she was not only pregnant, but also pregnant with twins. She was going to be bedridden for the last few months of her pregnancy. She was actually four months along and this meant that she wouldn't be able to lift and care for Bonnie's baby as well as if she was not pregnant. The doctors were very concerned that she was going to be bedridden for the last three months or risk the chance of having the babies delivered prematurely. At this point she wasn't sure what to do. Her heart was telling her to go ahead and adopt Bonnie's baby, knowing that this was a sure thing and that she would be helping a baby as well. On the other hand, her logic was telling her that this was going to be too much and that she

45

could end up risking the lives of the babies that she was carrying. Needless to say, I was shocked. She asked my opinion and as much as I wanted for her to be able to adopt this baby, it didn't look to be the wisest decision for everyone involved.

By the time she left my home, we both realized that even though we only had a few days until "D" day (delivery), the best thing to do was try to find new families for Bonnie to consider. I wanted to have two or three families ready to meet Bonnie so she wouldn't have any time to worry.

At this point I needed to leave and pick up Bonnie and Jason at the airport. Now, with my large family I wouldn't be able to leave them all with Dave, so I had four of my little ones in tow. They loved the trips we would make to the airport, as it was always an adventure. We really looked like a flock, with a mommy duck and her babies following behind. Needless to say, I didn't need to hold a sign up. We were pretty obvious. Bonnie would know from my little group, which was the Project Cuddle Club. I had no idea what she looked like; only that she was very pregnant and had a little boy with her. As people began to deplane we noticed a couple of pregnant girls, but they were traveling together. A little boy with beautiful brown curly hair came running towards us between the passengers. He had a little plastic plane in his hand and seemed to be pretending that he was flying it through the terminal. It took about another minute for a very weary looking young lady to appear through the crowd. I knew by the panicked look on her face that this had to be Bonnie. I caught Jason as he flew by us. The kids all laughed, but Jason was put into instant shock. He didn't know who I was or where his mommy was. Bonnie relaxed and smiled as she saw that Jason was in good hands now. She had all the symptoms of most of our girls. She didn't even waddle as she walked; I could barely tell that she was pregnant. "Hi Bonnie," I shouted, as she got closer. "How'd ya know it was me?" She hollered. By then we had "met" and I gave her a big hug and she hugged me right back. An instant bond was formed.

Bonnie was a tough little cookie. She had previously been an M.P. in the Navy. She was only five feet and two inches tall, but what she lacked in height, she made up for in her attitude. She hoisted Jason onto her hip and then told us that she only had her carry-on bag, so we wouldn't need to go down to the baggage claim area. I asked Bejay to help carry the bag for her, but Bonnie insisted on carrying it herself.

We made our way down to the "Cuddle Van," and started our journey towards home. I knew I was going to have to bring up the subject very soon about her talking to new families, but I wasn't looking forward to it. I decided that rather than wait, I would try and tell Bonnie now about this new situation. This way she would have enough time that day to at least speak with a few different families.

Surprisingly Bonnie took this unexpected news very well. I explained that we had new families who would love to speak with her right away. She really didn't care at that point who was going to take the baby as long as they took it. I arranged for one family to come over for dinner and another to meet us at Chuck E. Cheese for dessert. It was raining outside, so we tried to be creative; we decided to put a red-and-white checkered tablecloth down on the living room floor and invited the first family in for an old-fashioned picnic. They were a cute couple named John and Susan Walker. They had adopted once before and their little daughter Katie, who was three years old, was with them. She was quite a little young lady. She was the type who liked the ruffled dresses and hair bows. She was every mother's dream for a daughter.

We finished up our picnic and thanked the Walker family for coming. We piled everyone into the Cuddle Van and headed towards Chuck E. Cheese. Needless to say, the kids were in heaven. First they had a picnic and now this. Jason had never been to a place like this. He was in shock for the first few minutes but then warmed up and he had a wonderful time and enjoyed what every little boy should.

I knew that Bonnie wasn't completely happy with the Walkers, but she was very polite to them. I hoped that this second family would be a bit better. I think a part of the problem was she had never wanted a man involved in this whole situation. She had really been happy with the first woman she had chosen. I thought that this family might be a better one for her because the father was an older, gentler man. He was twenty years the senior of his wife. He adored her and they had been married for almost fourteen years. The one thing missing in their lives was a child. Now, they hoped that this would be their chance for a complete family. They tried through social services, but were turned down because of his age.

As we lifted Jason into the bounce room, I saw Karen and Tom Sampson walking through the front door. They made a handsome couple and though there was an age difference, it didn't seem to matter. They were truly in love. I went over to greet them and then brought them to Bonnie. She said "Hello" to them, and then went over to check on Jason. After she saw that he was doing fine without her direct attention, she came back and sat down at the table next to me. Karen and Tom sat across from us and nervously smiled, not sure what they should say or do. I tried to lighten the conversation and asked her to tell them about her flight. Within minutes I could tell that they had all begun to relax and form a bond. I wouldn't be surprised if this was the family she picked. There was just such sweetness about Tom and a sparkle in his big green eyes. I thought that he wouldn't be a threat in any way to Bonnie's child or to anyone else.

The Sampsons brought a little something for Jason. Bonnie had to pry him away from the bounce room in order to have him meet the Sampsons. Once he came over, he immediately attached himself to Tom. Bonnie caught on to this and realized that this was a different kind of man than she was used to. I knew by her expression that she had made her decision.

We finished our conversation and then gathered up all the children. On the way home I asked Bonnie what she was thinking. She told me that she had seriously looked the two families over and didn't want to see any others. She was sure of the family she was going to choose. We went into the living room as soon as we got home. I sat at my desk and she sat back on the "Bette sofa" (It was given to me by Bette Midler.). We talked about Bonnie's concerns and then how she wanted to proceed with telling the family she had chosen. I asked her if she wanted me to call the Sampsons and let them know she thought they would be the best family to care for and adopt her newborn baby. She said that she wanted to do it herself. I handed her the phone and gave her a piece of paper containing all the numbers. She dialed their cell phone number and waited for them to pick it up. On the third ring Tom answered the line. Bonnie said, "Hello Tom, this is Bonnie. How would you and Karen like to be parents?" She giggled as Tom shouted, "We're gonna be parents!" so loud that she had to pull the phone away from her ear. She was so relieved. She knew this was the right choice. I was willing to bet that even though the Sampsons weren't going to get any sleep tonight, Bonnie would sleep better than she had in months.

August 17, 1997

The following day the Sampson's attorney gave us instructions on where to go and what to do. We were in rush mode. We figured that we only had a week according to Bonnie's calculations, but the doctor wasn't as optimistic. He was willing to let her continue the pregnancy for up to two more weeks. He didn't want to take a chance that the baby's lungs wouldn't be completely developed. This could definitely be an issue if it was delivered prematurely.

For the next few days we kept Bonnie and her son busy. She got a big kick out of our little Jonathon. Though he was only four years old, he acted as though he were thirty. I didn't want her to sit around and get bored or depressed, so we transferred the crisis line to the cell phone and took Bonnie and Jason on the ferry down to the Newport Beach Pavilion. I even answered a crisis call in the Cuddle Van while the children and Bonnie got out of the car and stood on the deck of the ferry as we crossed the bay.

Bonnie got along very well with all our children. Bejay our ten year old, loved to tease her and she teased him right back. Once when we were driving downtown, Jonathon was seated next to Bonnie. She was laughing over something he had said. She said,

"You're just a little bon-bon." He stopped giggling and looked Bonnie straight in the eye. "My name isn't Bon-Bon. It's Jonnie… Where did you get the idea for Bon-Bon?" Bonnie couldn't believe his spunky response.

August 20, 1997

It was Thursday evening and Bonnie wasn't feeling very well. We decided we should go to bed early just in case she was going into labor. Sure enough, at around one in the morning Bonnie came to me and told me that she was indeed having contractions, and they were about ten minutes apart. I called the doctor and he advised us to get to the hospital right away, as he did not want her delivering just yet. Since she hadn't gotten proper prenatal care we just couldn't be sure of the due date. We drove the twenty minutes to the hospital and went in through the emergency entrance. They hooked Bonnie up to the monitors and found that sure enough, she was having contractions. The doctor then ordered an injection that would hopefully slow them down and then stop them all together. Bonnie wasn't happy about that, but said that she would be willing to try it if they felt it was absolutely necessary.

Four hours later the contractions had stopped and we were allowed to go home. They told us that if she started contracting again we should come back. If she were dilated to four or greater, they would admit her and then deliver. Bonnie told me under her breath that there was no way she was coming back to the hospital unless she was delivering. She had been very agitated by the drugs they had given her, and wasn't about to let them give her any more.

As we began to walk out of the labor and delivery unit, Bonnie gently reached over and grabbed my wrist and squeezed. Very quietly she said, "Stop please." I think she was afraid that someone else would hear what she was saying. I stopped in the middle of the hall and asked, "Are you?" and she nodded yes. She was having another contraction. She wanted to go out to the car. I asked her if she was sure about that, and she was. She wanted me to believe in her and that she knew her due date better than anyone else. We kept on going towards the exit and helped her get into the van.

Bonnie would get to go back home and relax with her little son by her side.

As Bonnie rested, I caught up on a bit of work and made the kids' breakfast. It was only seven in the morning but we had been up most of the night. Now, I would be getting them all ready for school.

By two in the afternoon, Bonnie was really beginning to have some major contractions. I found her squatting on my sofa. Now, it was about to become a delivery table for Bonnie's baby if we didn't get her convinced to go back to the hospital very soon. She was so afraid of having to get another shot that she refused to go until she knew she was too far along for them to refuse her. I was beginning to work up a sweat just watching her. I begged and pleaded with her and called our friend Shirley Yankie and told her what was going on. By this point the contractions were only two minutes apart and we had to go right to the hospital. I had been keeping track of the contractions on a legal note pad and brought it with me as I coaxed Bonnie off of my sofa. I couldn't believe that her water hadn't broken while she was squatting there.

Finally, we were in the Cuddle Van and on our way up the free-way. Bonnie was starting to have back contractions while I was driving. I would write down the time that each one started and then rub her back while driving down the freeway. As we got within a block of the hospital, she told me that she needed to push. That was the last straw. I picked up the cell phone and called over to the doctor's office. They would have a gurney on hand for Bonnie as we rounded the corner. "Oh God it hurts!" Bonnie yelled as I con-tinued to write down the time and then kept rubbing the small of her back. We pulled into the emergency room unloading area and honked the horn. Two attendants ran out and lifted Bonnie onto a gurney. She told the nurses that she needed to push. They told her the same thing I had said, "You will have to wait." They ran her back to the labor and delivery unit while I parked the van.

I rushed past many of the nurses with whom I had so often worked. Two of them got very busy hooking Bonnie up to monitors and an IV. Bonnie looked at me with all seriousness and said, "I can't do this!" I think that if I had been close enough for her to reach me, she would have grabbed me by the shirt collar. I looked at her and said, "Well honey, it's too late to back up this truck." The nurses laughed. I held her hand as they checked to see how far along she was: "Dilated to nine!" With that little bit of information, I tried to encourage Bonnie, but she wasn't buying it. She wanted some pain medicine and she wanted it NOW! Unfortunately, she was so far dilated that they couldn't give her anything. I let the nurse deliver that news while I gowned up for the delivery.

We had put a call into the adoptive parents-to-be, Karen and Tom. They had been down during her contractions in the middle of the night and then left because it looked as if it was going to be a week or so longer. We left a message and would hope they would get here before the baby was born. Bonnie didn't want to be the one holding it after it was born. She wanted Karen and Tom to be on hand while she pushed. There was no sign of the Sampson family.

I was the lucky one to be able to watch as this baby entered the world. I had my camera with me and placed it to the side of her pillow. Every time she would push, I would help her by lifting the pillow. I heard the doctor say, "Give one more push Bonnie. I can see its hair!" He had really hoped that she would wait another couple of weeks since we couldn't be sure about the due date, but at least now he helped in cheering her on to the end of her pregnancy.

I peeked over and saw a head full of red hair. Soon the shoulders were delivered and I found out that Bonnie had a son. "What is it? What is it?" she asked. I told her it was a boy. I asked her if she wanted to see the baby. "No, not right now. I'll do that later." I stood by her for the next half hour while the doctors took care of her. Being the tough little M.P., she wasn't about to let down her guard and cry. I left her side just long enough to call in a volunteer who brought her son Jason up to see her.

By the time I came back, they had weighed rescue baby #77 and measured him. It's a good thing he didn't go any longer. He was 9 lbs. 2 oz. and 21 inches long. He had Bonnie's lips and eyes. I wished that Tom and Karen had been able to see this.

Bonnie was moved to a different floor so that she wouldn't have to hear the cries of babies, especially hers. Once we got her settled in, I asked her what she was craving. She told me banana cream pie, pancakes and a bacon cheeseburger. Bonnie took a few minutes and developed a plan. As soon as the Sampson family went to labor and delivery they were to be instructed to come up to her room. She wanted to be the one to tell them that they were parents.

About ten minutes after arriving in her new room, Karen and Tom arrived at the hospital. They had no idea that the baby had already been born. They had stopped by the labor and delivery area and were instructed to come up to Bonnie's room. No one told them anything. They both had a fearful look on their face as they entered Bonnie's room. I think that they were afraid that since they did not get to go into the nursery, perhaps Bonnie had changed her mind.

Bonnie saw the fear in their eyes and was excited that she had the control to turn that fear into joy. "Come on in," Bonnie said in a cheery, reassuring voice. "Are you okay?" Tom asked. "I'm fine. Congratulations, you have a son." Karen put her purse down on the extra bed and ran over to embrace her hero—the mother of her child. "I can't believe it!" Karen cried and embraced Bonnie. Tom came over and placed his lips against Bonnie's forehead and gave her a gentle kiss. "Thank you so much. Our lives are now complete." This gentle man was so thankful for what Bonnie had done for him, for his wife and for their son.

"Now, I want you guys to go down with Debbe and let her take pictures of you seeing him for the first time," Bonnie stated. "Not a problem!" Tom chimed in. I said, "Then, you need to order this young lady something to eat. She's decided on pancakes, banana cream pie and a bacon cheeseburger." They both laughed. "What ever she wants," Karen said as she chuckled.

I went downstairs to see the newest member of the Sampson

family. He was so cute. Tom was scrubbing up and was so serious. Karen could hardly wait. She had waited so very long for this moment. I snapped photos while the baby squinted. I asked them if they had chosen a name yet. They told me that his name would be Jeffrey, after Karen's father. He had passed away when she was a little girl, but she always promised herself that someday she would have a son and that would be his name. So, Jeffrey Sampson was now in the arms of his new mother.

I went back upstairs and kept Bonnie company for a while. Tom came back upstairs and asked if he should go and get the food for Bonnie. I told him I would place the order over the phone and it would probably be done in about twenty minutes. He then asked Bonnie if there was anything else that she needed. "No, I just want to see Jason." As she smiled I could tell she was beginning to get very tired. So was I. I told her that I had ordered a kid's meal for Jason and they could have lunch together.

After leaving the hospital, Bonnie laid on the sofa for the next few days. It was hard after that to keep her down. We began to plan her farewell to Jeffrey. She decided that she wanted to have a baby dedication at our home. We began to make a list of whom she wanted to invite. Bonnie had become close to a few wonderful volunteers and my mommy, Scotty. Another girl had been in our program at the same time as Bonnie. Though that girl had delivered her baby and then given it up for adoption, the adoptive family, the Gentlys, had gotten to be friends with Bonnie.

August 29, 1997

Saturday morning came, and I found Bonnie in the kitchen starting to prepare snacks. She had insisted on purchasing them herself. It was so cute. She decorated paper plates and placed lunchmeats, cheeses and breads on them. She also had desserts. Our pastor from Rock Harbor Church performed a little ceremony. It was beautiful. I knew that Tom and Karen were extremely nervous because they were afraid that if they came, Bonnie might change her mind after seeing the baby and want to keep him. I knew that this wasn't even a thought in her mind. They agreed to come and in turn, Bonnie promised to sign a waver so that she would no longer have any rights to her son. It would be signed the following day. In fact, Tom was going to take her to have it signed. Then they were going to tour Hollywood. It was a nice way to end a very emotional day.

At noon, everyone began to arrive. My mother is always early, so of course, she was the first to arrive. The pastor arrived and took a few minutes to find out what Bonnie wanted to have done. He was so kind. The doorbell rang and when my daughter Lani answered the door, I saw that it was Tom and Karen who were at the entrance. They had brought extra everything. As they tried to maneuver the big, blue stroller over the threshold and into the house, I went into the living room to let Bonnie know they had arrived. I asked her how she was feeling. By the time I got this question out, the couple had already gotten to the edge of the living room carpet. Both Bonnie and I saw them at the same moment. There was the big, blue stroller at the edge of the living room carpet with Bonnie's son inside. She took one look and began to sob. That tough old M.P. finally cracked. She grabbed me and wept. I confess, I was crying too. I held her until she had a chance to catch her breath. I asked her if she wanted me to pick him up and hand him to her. That's what she wanted me to do.

Bonnie held Jeffrey as everyone around her wiped tears from their eyes. She went over to the "hofa" (Jonnie can't say sofa) and slowly sat down. She just gazed into his little eyes. He was so alert. I was amazed at how bright he was. Pudgula our cat, slept on top of the Xerox machine while the pastor began his dedication ceremony. We all gathered around Bonnie as we prayed. As we finished praying, Jason came in from outside. He stopped dead in his tracks when he saw his mother holding this strange creature. All of the sudden he burst out in tears. Everyone began to laugh as he threw himself into a major tantrum. Bonnie handed the baby over to Karen and began to console her son. We all shared positive affirmations about Bonnie and how she had touched our lives.

After everyone had shared and Jason calmed down, we all gathered around Karen and Tom. We then bowed our heads and prayed for this baby and his new family. After the ceremony we all went and enjoyed the meal that Bonnie had prepared.

✧✧ UPDATE ✧✧

Bonnie went home the following week. Jonathon became so attached to her, that he finally allowed her to call him "Bon-Bon". In fact, if you ask him his nickname that's the name he will give you. Bonnie knows she did what she had to do. She is now in college and will soon be graduating. Her family never found out what happened when she was out in California. I don't think she will ever tell them. It's our secret.

Recently I appeared on the "Oprah Show" and Bonnie was willing to share (behind a screen) her situation and the fact that she had gotten help from Project Cuddle. We are so proud of her. It wasn't easy, but because of her sharing, we have been able to help rescue more girls and their babies from abandonment.

Tom and Karen love Jeffrey so very much and are wonderful parents. They can't wait for Jeffrey to grow just a little bit more so he can go out and join his daddy for at least one of his four sets of tennis each day. "We can't imagine life without our Jeffrey," Karen said as she leaned over and kissed Jeffrey who was asleep in her arms.

Chapter Three

Good Girls Can
Get Pregnant

INTRODUCTION

So often people come to me and ask, "What kind of girls end up calling your line?" They are often surprised that many, many of these girls and women are considered to be highly educated and very caring. Some are the pillars of their local community and others are nursing students. The following chapter, "Good Girls Can Get Pregnant," will help you understand the types of "good girls" who end up in tragic situations and how we helped get them through safely.

The Amish Girl is Coming!

It's the 4th of July and the entire family is at the O'Brien home where we are celebrating my daughter Lani's 21st birthday. I had just received a phone call from one of the volunteers who was manning the crisis line and who had been corresponding on the internet with a fourteen-year old, pregnant Amish girl. We had tried for over a month to get this girl to call our toll-free number. She finally bought phone cards that she used when calling from pay phones to this volunteer. Now this young girl, Amy, had finally gotten up the courage to call and speak with me.

I knew I had to leave the party in order to switch the crisis line back to my home. I hated to leave, but I knew that this girl wanted to speak to me. The volunteer had told her I would be there in ten minutes. That was barely enough time to get to my house from the party.

I made it! And not a minute too soon. I had barely arrived home, and transferred the line when the phone rang. I was so nervous and yet so excited that she was finally calling. I gave my usual introduction and waited for her to say something. She didn't. I realized that I had better say something to her or she might hang up. "Amy, is that you?" I gently questioned. She was so very quiet, but I heard her say, "Yes." I felt myself starting to cry as I spoke, "Oh Amy...I'm so happy you called." She finally spoke, "Are you crying? I'm sorry. Did I make you mad?" I was startled and realized that I had better try to reassure her quickly that everything was all right. "Oh no sweetie. I'm crying because I'm happy. I'm happy because you finally called," I tried to reassure her, but it took some convincing. She finally understood. "If you were the tin man you would be rusted," she said. It took me a minute to understand what she was saying. "You're right Amy. You're pretty smart and funny too."

What started out as a few minutes of conversation, ended up a two-hour call. As we began to talk I learned a lot about this little girl from Pennsylvania. She and her mother had been living in the Amish community until she was three. Her father had died from a ruptured appendix when she was only two. Her mother had been raising her on her own until she met an Englishman whom she took a fancy to. This was something that was forbidden in their community. One day while out at the market, she came upon this handsome Englishman. They had stopped and talked so many times before, but this time they went off behind the market to talk. Someone in the community caught them holding hands. When she returned to her home that night, her bags were packed and by the door. Two heads of the Amish community came over and told her that she was no longer welcome in their community. She had shamed her family and her community.

Amy and her mother had to find a way to survive. Things would never be the same and it would not be easy. Amy told me that her mother worked for a large company in the city. She would work all day in a modern building with phones, computers, etc. and then go home to a much simpler life. For example: She would still can all her own vegetables and fruits. She would wash her clothing in the tub with cold water and there was no television in her home and Amy was forbidden to wear anything sleeveless.

Amy suffered the most with this way of life. It was as though two completely different ways of life were being inter-twined. She was sent to public school because her mother couldn't afford a private one. She hung around with average teens all day and learned about MTV, mini skirts, tattoos and piercings. Then she came home to kneading dough and no phones allowed in the house. I couldn't even imagine how difficult this must have been for her.

60

July 7, 1999

I remember a subsequent call that came in from Amy. It was 2 a.m. and she was in tears. I asked her what the problem was. She very quietly told me that she was in a lot of pain from being whipped. I asked her what she had done that was so terrible she should get punished like that. Her comment was that she had gone to see a movie. This wasn't allowed, even if it had been a Disney film. She told me how the cuts would bleed if she moved. She said, "Don't worry though, I'll just stand up tonight and tomorrow it should be better." Her mother had told her that she was "grounded till the undertaker comes." I felt so bad for her, but knew that she wasn't about to give us any help in finding out where she lived. There was no way to really help her at this time.

I asked her how she had been able to hide the pregnancy so long. She told me that she wore a girdle and baggy clothes. She said the girdle was getting very tight on her. She had revealed the story of how she got pregnant to only one person. This was the volunteer who had reported it to me. I already knew, but listened intently as she told me what had happened to her.

Amy had snuck out of her house in order to join her friends for a very large Halloween party. She had dressed as Alice in Wonderland. She didn't know most of the people there. Somehow, part way through the evening she ended up meeting a few teenage boys that seemed nice enough, and when they decided to go down to the basement for a couple games of pool she decided to join them. She doesn't remember most of that night, but she remembers that it was pretty dark, and once she was in the basement the guys locked the door. She tried to yell for help, but with the blaring music and brick walls, no one heard her. Three different teen boys raped her that night. When Amy snuck back into her bedroom, she collapsed. She never told anyone about that night until calling our phone operator. She said this was God's way of punishing her for being so bad. She had been so depressed whenever she thought about that night.

According to my calculations, she was due around July 25th.

61

That wasn't giving us much time to get her medical care and everything else we needed to do. When I asked her about seeing a doctor, she got upset. She said that she wasn't allowed to see a doctor because it was against her religion. She told me that she planned on delivering the baby at a hotel, alone. "If I die, that will be God's will," she stated. When I tried to confront her with the fact that there was a baby's life at risk as well, she told me that she knew that, but she wasn't going to a doctor.

Somehow, we needed to get her some help. My mind was working rapidly to try and come up with some way to help her. I asked her if she would be allowed to see a midwife. She thought about it and said that would probably be all right. I told her I would try to locate one and then let her know the next day.

Over the next few weeks other volunteers who took the crisis line and I would get calls from Amy. To our amazement we discovered that Amy had never seen a television show until 11 months before. For current events in school she was to watch the news and make daily reports based on the current issues. She had to beg her mother, until she eventually gave in. The rule was that it stayed in Amy's room and was only to be used for school projects. Well, just like any "normal" teen, that lasted about a week. When her mother was at work or out for some reason, the television would go on. It was a whole new world. She loved "Alvin and the Chipmunks," and "Happy Days."

During a conversation Amy got real serious and asked, "Was the big brother on 'Happy Days' shunned? He was shunned wasn't he?" At first I didn't understand what she was asking. I finally figured it out. Because he was only on the show for just a short time, she thought that he had been cast out or shunned. She actually thought this was a real life story. I tried not to laugh as I began explaining that what she was seeing on TV wasn't real. It seemed a very difficult thing for her to understand.

In the days ahead, we tried to work towards a safe solution for Amy and her unborn baby. I kept thinking about how she planned on delivering the baby alone.

Amy began to open up to the other volunteers who were answering the crisis line. Amy would go on for a good hour or more. She taught me a lot about her life and how different it was from the average teen's life. She wasn't allowed clothing that was sleeveless and they had to be quarter-length sleeves or longer. She did not get her first pair of jeans until she was in the 6th grade and T-shirts still were not allowed to be fitted. Once, not too long ago, she decided to cut her hair. She cut off two and a half feet of her beautiful brown hair: "My mom was so mad that I couldn't sit down for over three days after that whipping." She laughed when she told me that. It's as though she got a kick out of ticking her mother off.

Amy seemed quite star-struck. I would intermingle questions about her personal life with questions about TV trivia. I asked her who her favorite star was and she told me it was a boy she saw in a movie on TV. She said, "The movie is 'National Velvet.' His name is Mickey Rooney." I burst into laughter. "Oh honey, that movie was made a long, long time ago. He's been married at least six times." She was so surprised by that. Little things that we take for granted, she looked at so differently. She had just recently had her first can of soda. She told me, "I love the bubbles…they make me sneeze."

July 18, 1999

Once, about a week before she was due, she called and was really down. I had to talk to her for quite a while and pushed in order to get her to tell me what the problem was. Our conversation went on all the way into the wee hours of the morning. She had sneaked out to see the new release of "American Pie." When she returned home her mother confronted her. She told her the truth, and then had been whipped so severely that she was bleeding on her buttocks. She said, "I've been slimed just like the Ghost Busters." I asked her what that meant, and I was told that her panties had been sticking to her bloody whip marks. She had made an old fashion remedy that was a mixture of herbs and something similar to Vaseline and then applied it over the wounds. She had seen a cartoon at a neighbor's house that showed the Ghost Busters being "slimed" by the ghosts. I felt so helpless because I couldn't find her in order to help her more. Finally, at around three in the morning, she fell asleep. I could hear her breathing on the other end of the phone. I hesitantly hung up the phone and hoped that she would have at least a few minutes of painless sleep.

The following morning, she called the crisis line at around 7:30 a.m. She asked me one of the strangest questions that I had ever heard. "Do you think the baby could have a cold?" I asked her why she suspected that and was told that she had a discharge that looked like mucus or "boogers" as she called them, laced with some blood. I explained that this was her mucus plug. That was a warning sign that she was close to delivering. Now, I was really getting nervous.

I again offered the phone number of the midwife that we had located. This woman was willing to go anywhere in the state in order to help her. I had asked her about talking with some families that were interested in meeting her or at least talking with her on the phone. It would then be up to her to find a solution that she could live with.

Amy contacted the midwife and began to form a relationship that would come in handy in the weeks to come. They talked about all kinds of things. She was filled with questions like, "Why is it called a cell phone?" and "How come people don't wear their underwear to the beach? There's more material on them than in the swim suit."

On one of the last conversations I had with her before her due date, she said, "Zeus swallowed his siblings. He had a really, really bad headache and someone cracked open his head and found all the siblings...they were all full grown. Why can't I deliver like Zeus?" I could understand her frustration. She didn't ask for this. At one point she had threatened to give birth at the hospital and then jump off a bridge. "I might as well jump, my mother is going to kill me anyway." Her wounds had begun to heal, but she told me that she was still putting salt water on them in order to help them heal and keep from getting infected.

July 21, 1999

Amy was finally realizing that this baby was going to come and she had better come up with a plan. She talked to two families and then met with the midwife. Three days later, she delivered. The midwife delivered a small, but healthy little boy. He was only 5 lbs. 4 oz., but was able to breathe quite well on his own. The midwife called the family that Amy had chosen to have rescue her baby. Fortunately, the family Amy decided to work with lived only thirty minutes away. They would arrive before the baby had even gotten his first bath.

✧✧ UPDATE ✧✧

I regret that I never got to meet Amy. I know that the experience was both traumatic and life changing. Her son is now in a modern American home. He will have electricity, and his mother will do the laundry in a washing machine. Amy still sees him once a year for his birthday. Amy is now finishing her senior year and will be going to college on a scholarship. Upon finishing, she hopes to be a children's counselor. She would like to help abused children and feels that she would be able to understand their pain better than the average person. Though her mother will probably never know her secret, Amy proved to herself that there was a way out of this deep, dark hole. We are just so thankful that she called. Now, she and little Nathan James are truly living life.

My Ohio Sunshine

Spring had sprung. Not only were the birds and bees providing babies for planet earth, but girls and women were also a busy group that would be providing many, many babies throughout the country. Ricki Lake shared our toll free number with the viewing audience and our crisis line began to ring off the hook. One particular young lady who truly touched my heart was Michelle.

February 10, 1999

Michelle had called our crisis line. She was very quiet on the phone. I asked her if she needed help. I could barely hear her reply, but she did say, "Yes." I began to learn about Michelle's situation. She was only sixteen years old. She was about eight months along and had told no one. "No one can ever find out," she said. I began asking her what options she felt she would be comfortable with and she told me the only one she wanted was to find a way to get rid of the baby. She didn't want it to be in her home state. She began to tell me about the father of the baby. I explained that he would have to know and sign off if he wasn't interested in raising it. I found out that the baby was going to be part Native American. This was going to present a new set of problems. There is a Federal Law that states that only families of Native American ancestry can adopt Native American babies. This wasn't going to be easy. I tried to encourage her to tell her family. There was just no way that she was going to do that. I just hoped that there was enough time for us to get this all figured out before the baby delivered. I called a wonderful attorney by the name of Steven Lazarus who sits on the Board of Directors and specializes in adoption. I asked him to find out some of the legal issues involved in this case. I always know that he will not only find the right answers, but he truly cares.

I wouldn't hear from Michelle for over a week. I called her and found out that she still hadn't talked to her family or her boyfriend. She had no plans in doing so. I explained to her about her options for medical help, etc., and she then told me that she wanted to have families lined up that she could talk to. I got a volunteer involved; Michelle was happy to have someone to talk with.

February 24, 1999

The next week was spent trying to make sure that we had everything in order. We were finally able to get Michelle to go to her older sister and tell her about the pregnancy. Michelle went home after revealing her secret and started a warm bath. She needed to relax before she and her sister Tawny confronted their mother. As Michelle looked into the bathroom mirror at herself the bathroom door suddenly swung open and in walked her mother. Michelle froze. She didn't know what to expect. "Michelle, show me your stomach," her mother calmly requested. Michelle could tell that she was in total disbelief. She complied and slowly lifted her blouse to reveal a swelling belly. Though her stomach was larger than normal, there was no way that she looked as though she was due in the next three to four weeks. Tawny, realizing that her mother had gone into the bathroom after she spilled the beans ahead of schedule, stood behind her mother and heard her say, "Oh my gosh, you are pregnant." Neither Michelle nor her mother could move. "I guess you know, huh?" Michelle said very sheepishly as she looked down toward the floor.

It only took a few more seconds and Tawny realized that she needed to be the one that broke the ice in this conversation. She said, "Sorry Sis. I figured it would be easier if I told her when we were alone. She didn't believe me though."

Michelle, Tawny and their mother talked for the next twenty minutes. Then they picked up the phone and called the crisis line. I took the call that night. "Hi Debbe, this is Michelle. My Mom wants to talk to you." I was so surprised. "You mean she knows?"

68

I questioned. "Yah, she just found out." I spoke with this woman as she tried to absorb what she had just learned. The reaction that this poor woman had was very similar to that of someone who had just won a couple of million dollars in the lottery. She began to talk about how she wanted to support her daughter through this time, then in the middle of a sentence she spoke her thought, "Oh my gosh, that's why she's been so irritable lately!" We went on for the next few minutes in conversation and then she popped up with another thought. She said, "Oh, I had noticed that she had gained some weight, so I was going to go out and buy her some diet foods and start her on a walking program with me." It was incredible to hear this all unfold in front of me.

I told her how very proud I was of how she was responding and her willingness to stick by her daughter through whatever her daughter decided. I could only wish that so many other parents who find themselves in similar situations would handle it just as well.

Over the next few days Michelle and her mother would begin to talk about what they were going to do. Michelle was going to go to the doctor and find out just how far along she really was. I got a call from Michelle that following week. "Hi Debbe, it's me, Michelle. Well, my mom and I went out yesterday and picked out the wallpaper. It's really pretty. It's going to be a girl," she announced.

Michelle and her mother had decided to raise the baby that was about to be born. I was so relieved to know that she had gotten medical treatment and the baby was going to be raised by a family that really cared. Though I would still be concerned about Michelle, I didn't feel nearly the amount of pressure that I had before.

I checked in on her once in a while during those next few weeks. I was happy to hear that she was progressing well in her pregnancy and that the boyfriend was now aware of the pregnancy that had been such a secret only a couple of weeks ago. He planned on getting involved in his baby's life once she was born. Things were definitely looking up from where they were a month ago. I honestly believe that once girls like Michelle share their secret with someone like Project Cuddle, they become accountable. That secret was no longer hers alone. We now shared it. For this I was very thankful.

March 8, 1999

Finally, the day came and she delivered the most beautiful little baby. Michelle's mother had been present at the birth, as was the wonderful sister who helped tell her secret. Alexa Jade was safe in the arms of her loving family, as rescue baby #199.

✧✧   UPDATE   ✧✧

I finally got to meet my little ray of sunshine from Ohio. I was filming the Montel Williams Show and during one segment, Montel asked a young woman, "You were pregnant and hid your pregnancy. You found an organization to call and they helped you. Do you remember what her name was?" Michelle stood up and said, "Yes, it was Debbe." Montel asked, "What was her last name?" Michelle told him that she didn't know the lady's last name. Montel said, "Well, we have that woman here today. Her name is Debbe Magnusen. She's the founder of Project Cuddle, the organization you called." I had been trying to hold back the tears when I realized who she was. I stood up and went towards her, we cried as we embraced. I was so proud of her. She was so beautiful. A tall blonde with sparkling eyes. It was hard to imagine that she had just given birth two months before. After the show, we met back stage and she gave me a photo of herself and her new little one. She had the high cheekbones of a Native American and beautiful dark black hair. Though I had previously refused to fly in an airplane, I was now very happy I had faced my fear. Seeing her was worth everything.

Little Miss Virgin Isles

April 3, 1998

It was only 3:00a.m. when I got a call from Rachel. The tiny voice on the other end of the phone line was so faint that I questioned whether there really was someone there. I thought that perhaps I was dreaming. I asked, "Could you please speak up? I can barely hear you." The person on the other end of the line cleared their throat and then she spoke, "I'm sorry. Can you hear me now?" I reassured her that she could now be heard and began asking how we could help her.

She proceeded to tell me that she was in the Virgin Isles and didn't know if we would be able to help her since she was so far away. I explained that we could help her even if she was in a different country. Project Cuddle has no barriers.

As her story began to unfold, I learned that she was from a very prominent family on her island. Her mother held a government position and was known by most everyone around. Her father was the head of the labor and delivery unit at the island's hospital. She was a straight "A" student and had already been offered a full scholarship to Yale. She and her boyfriend, Thomas, were very heavily involved in the Catholic Church. Neither had ever been intimate with anyone else. They were very well respected by the locals and everyone expected them to go far in life. They had their futures planned. Rachel would go to the mainland and get her law degree. Thomas would stay on the island and work as an apprentice in his father's business. One day he would be a partner and could financially care for his family if Rachel wanted to take time

71

off from work to rear their children.

Their original plan had been to wait until after the wedding to consummate their marriage. Somehow they found themselves alone one evening and went further than they had ever planned on going. Rachel had never even entertained the idea that she could be pregnant. After all, she and Thomas had slept together only that one time. They both felt so guilty and mutually agreed to wait until they got married. It had been six months since that incident took place.

After learning about Project Cuddle on television, Rachel decided that perhaps she should call. She didn't think that she could possibly be pregnant because they had only been together that one time, but she hadn't had a period for over four months. She got butterflies in the pit of her stomach as she dialed the number. The first time she dialed, she stayed on the line just long enough to hear me say the first four words. I felt so helpless. I could only hope that she would call back again.

While I waited for her to call back, I kept my mind busy by doing chores. My dear husband Dave came into the kitchen when he smelled the brownies baking. Dave was always so happy when he smelled them. He came over and gave me a big hug and kiss. As we stood there enjoying the aroma of the brownies and momentary silence, little Jonathon came in and patted me on the leg and then said, "Snap out of it you guys." Dave and I cracked up. The littlest member of the family was certainly making himself known.

Finally, the phone rang again and this time Rachel stayed on the line. I spoke with her for almost an hour. She asked me if it was true that she couldn't get pregnant the first time she had sex. I explained that this was an old wives' tale and that she could be pregnant. She was devastated when she heard that. "What should I do? Oh my gosh. My parents will kill me. There's no way I can let them know. Their reputations are so important to them. I think I'm going to be sick," she declared. I told her to take a deep breath and try to relax.

I tried to get her mind off herself. "Hey, Rachel let me tell you what my son Jonathon did." She silently waited on the other end of the line. I figured I would probably be able to get her distracted long enough to get her to calm down. I went on to tell her that my four-year-old son had been seriously talking to me about his fear of growing old. I explained that he didn't need to worry. He wasn't going to shrivel up and get old for a long time.

Well, we got a Jacuzzi installed about a week ago and yesterday Jonathon stayed in there for almost two hours. When he got out, he went in to shower and dry off. All of a sudden he came out hysterically screaming, "I don't want to die! I'm turning into an old man!" I couldn't figure out what was going on. I finally got him to quit crying long enough to tell me what was wrong. He showed me his wrinkled hands and whimpered as he said, "See, I'm shriveling up."

Rachel laughed. It was great to hear her laugh. At this point I was still running the crisis line from my living room. Jonathon came in and I asked him if he would like to say hello to Rachel. He said, "Sure." He grabbed the phone from my hand and began a two-minute conversation. When I got the phone back, Rachel thanked me for helping her through this tough time. She promised me that she would go to a clinic the following morning and have a pregnancy test done. I gave her the name and address of a clinic that wasn't in the immediate area she lived, hoping she would be able get the results without bumping into anyone she knew.

April 4, 1998

I got a call from Rachel that following afternoon. Rachel was in tears as she told me that she was indeed pregnant. "This is going to ruin everything." She had an ultrasound and found out that she was six months along. She didn't want to keep it and she didn't want to forfeit her scholarship to Yale. She knew she was extremely talented and she wanted to use that talent. This baby was a gift from God, she told me, but she wasn't ready to accept this gift.

I encouraged her to speak with Thomas and tell him what was

73

going on. She was willing to do this, but wouldn't even consider telling her parents. I didn't hear from her for almost three weeks, but when I did, it was under very different circumstances.

April 25, 1998

"Debbe, it's Rachel. I'm in the hospital." she said. Her voice was really weak and slow. She told me that she had been driving home from church and was broadsided by a drunk driver. She had been pinned in the car and had to be airlifted to the hospital. She was getting really good treatment since her dad was the head of the labor and delivery department. The staff had tried their best to keep the accident and the pregnancy a secret from Rachel's parents. So far, they had been able to accomplish this. The baby seemed to be doing well considering what both Rachel and her unborn baby had just gone through.

Rachel suffered a broken leg and one broken rib due to the accident. She was in a lot of pain and she began to worry about the baby. It was the first time I heard her talk about the baby she had inside her. I realized that this was a turning point for her. Though she wasn't ready to spill the beans about this pregnancy to her parents, she sounded as though she was at least headed in that direction. She planned on telling them about the accident, but not until she was released from the maternity floor. She knew that her parents would be mad at her for keeping the accident a secret, but she was willing to face their wrath as opposed to hearing what they would say when they heard that they were about to become grandparents.

I called Rachel at the hospital each morning and evening until she was released. After the pain subsided, she planned on looking into families that would be willing to adopt the baby. We still had a couple of months before she was due, so the pressure wasn't as great as we usually had when some of our girls and women come to us while in active labor or just a week before.

I got another call from Rachel. She had been out of the hospital for three days now. She was in tears again. I asked her if she was crying because she was in pain. She told me that this wasn't the problem. Thomas, the father of the baby, had cheated on her and also gotten another girl pregnant. Mr. Perfect wasn't perfect any longer. She was heartbroken, as well as angry. There was no way she wanted to keep this baby now. She would show him. He would suffer for this mistake. His first-born child would be adopted out and he would never see it again. At least that's what she was planning when she called that day.

Rachel had been through so much over the past few months. I only wished that I lived closer so that I could help her face-to-face. I found a priest in her area that she was willing to speak with. He had a great reputation and a wonderful, big heart. I knew that she needed to go and see him before she even considered what to do about the future of herself and the baby. Over the next month, Rachel would meet with Father John two to three times a week. He helped her as she told her family about the hidden pregnancy. Though it was hard for them to accept, they loved their daughter and were willing to help her in raising this baby.

Rachel still didn't want to keep this baby, but her parents were insistent upon it. She felt so trapped. All she wanted to do was to get to college. Her love life was now shattered and her hopes and dreams for the future had all seemed to disappear with this pregnancy. She didn't know how she would ever be able to get through this.

She continued to meet with the priest for counseling and called me almost every day. She needed that support from someone who was not going to judge her or tell her that she was making the wrong decision.

In June, I began helping my oldest daughter, Lani as she planned her Fourth of July wedding. In order to maintain the crisis line and get the wedding done, I purchased a cell phone and took the crisis line with me whenever I went out. After an entire year of being confined to the house in order to take crisis calls, this was a wonderful and welcoming change. I got calls from Rachel at the floral wholesaler, the bridal shop and even at the tuxedo shop. She was getting close to delivery and getting very scared. The doctors told her that she had placenta-previa and would need to deliver via a C-section. This was the icing on the cake. She told me that she felt as though God was punishing her for her sin.

July 3, 1998

I purchased the flowers for Lani's wedding the day before the big event. We took them over to my girlfriend's house where the ceremony would take place and began to make the centerpieces. Thank goodness for that cell phone. In the midst of all the fern and flowers the phone began to ring. I knew it had to be her. Sure enough, she called to tell me that she had gotten toxemia and had to go to the hospital. They weren't sure if they were going to schedule the C-section for today or tomorrow. I put the last touches on another bouquet as we finished up our conversation.

July 4, 1998

It was a beautiful day for a wedding. I didn't hear anything from Rachel and when I called her home, no one answered. The sun was brightly shining and everything seemed to be moving along quite well. The only problem we ran into was that we couldn't purchase any hydrangeas for Lani and the bridesmaid's bouquets. This was her favorite flower and the main flower of the bouquets. I sent my girlfriend and my father out on a hydrangea hunt. Within thirty minutes, I was designing all five bouquets with blue and lavender hydrangeas. They had located homes in the neighborhood that were growing these gorgeous flowers and paid to cut them from their gardens.

I passed the cell phone to my dear friend and right arm, Kalei, while the ceremony began. I hoped that we would be able to get through the whole event without it ringing. Being a sentimental old fool, I began to cry as Lani's best friend and maid of honor sang.

I'd watched them both grow up and now my first was leaving the nest. Jonathon and Tyler were ring bearers in the ceremony and though Tyler took the whole thing very seriously, Jonathon did not. In a way it was a blessing because his dancing around and wiggling got me to smiling and my tears disappeared. It was a good thing that he had fake rings on his pillow.

We went on with the dinner and then promptly at 9:00 p.m. the cake was cut. The atmosphere was perfect. Everyone came outside to eat cake while looking out onto the bay. There were four professional displays of fireworks going on simultaneously. As we all watched the finale the cell phone began to ring. It was Rachel. She had delivered a son. When I asked her what she had named him, she told me that she hadn't. I knew from the tone in her voice that she wasn't in love with him or the thought of being his mother. I told her, "Sweetie, I want you to do me a favor. If you don't feel that you can love him and name him, then you need to find someone who will." She promised me that she would seriously look at him and her options, and let me know within two days what she had decided.

July 6, 1998

Rachel called and checked in as promised. She sounded much better. She had taken time to get to know her son. She realized that this WAS something she could do and wanted to do. She named rescue baby #19 Brandon Jacob after her father. He had come full circle and was willing to help her in the raising of his grandson.

✧✧ UPDATE ✧✧

It has been over two years since Rachel delivered her son. I got a call from her last September and she is now on the U.S. mainland attending Yale. She is so happy with the decisions she made and thrilled to be able to get on with her education. Her parents are helping her raise little Brandon and she sees him whenever she gets a chance. She is doing wonderfully well with her schooling and hopes to take her bar exam soon and then go back to the Island where she will set up her practice.

Chapter Four

The Weather Doesn't Help

INTRODUCTION

Most people have no idea that many girls and women we work with are dealing with issues in their personal lives, but may also be dealing with other elements. In the "The Weather Doesn't Help" stories that follow, you will learn how weather caused an extra set of problems for these women. In having to deal with both at the same time, it definitely kept us on our toes.

The Pajama Baby

February 14, 2000

It was Valentine's Day and we were having a little family get together with all seven children. Tyler, aka "Costume Boy," had found a new way to make money. He had taken a banana box and placed all kinds of things in it that he hoped to sell. There was everything from light bulbs to paper plates including a bottle of glitter and some extra doilies he had found lying around. He had attached a rope to the front and back of it on either side and then stepped into the middle of it. Only Tyler was tiny enough to fit in the center of this 7 x 10 ¾-inch opening. He instantly turned himself into the family vendor. To top it off, he wore a yellow beret with the words "Buy It From Me" scotch taped onto the brim, so that he would "look" more professional as he put it. He didn't like the fact that he wasn't having much luck with sales, so he headed toward the refrigerator. I knew exactly what he was hoping to do. Inside was a beautiful strawberry trifle that he wanted to offer as one of his items. As he reached for the door of the fridge, I called out "Vendor Man, can I please buy a light bulb?" I paid for the bulb and then he watched as I asked our middle daughter, Beth to bring the strawberry trifle out for the family. The time had come to serve dessert and open our valentines.

In the midst of this Valentine party we were temporarily interrupted by a crisis call on the hot-line. It was a young mother by the name of Tanisha. She had heard about us two weeks earlier on the Ricki Lake Show. When she initially called in a week earlier, I had taken the call. She was so frightened but knew that she wanted to leave the state and completely relocate with her two children. She guessed that she was almost seven months pregnant. I couldn't convince her to get any prenatal care, so I looked forward to having her relocate out to sunny California as soon as possible.

It didn't take long for my wish to come true. Tanisha's mother had evidently been suspicious that Tanisha had a problem or was in some kind of trouble. She had the codes for Tanisha's voice mail and decided to check the messages. Tanisha had forgotten that her mom had access to the codes and never thought anyone would hear the messages she had saved. One of the messages happened to be from a Rescue Family that Tanisha had requested to speak with. While Tanisha was out at the park, her mother was busy checking Tanisha's messages. When her mother heard the first message she was furious because of what she heard. She wanted to speak with Tanisha's father about the mess Tanisha had gotten into. Tanisha would be dealt with later that night.

They had just experienced the first snow of the season. There was a lot of excitement in the air and every child in town was at Central Park. They had a wonderful little hill there where JaeTee (age four) loved to sled. It was considered the one for beginners. Anneka (age two) wasn't too sure about all the snow, but she loved watching her big brother go down that hill. It had been a good day for Tanisha and the children. She wanted nothing more than to have dinner and then go and get a nice hot bath for herself and the children. She planned on settling down with some hot cocoa and a good book after tucking the kids in. Everything seemed normal at dinnertime. Tanisha told her family about their day and how she had taken Anneka and JaeTee to the park.

After helping to clear the dishes, Tanisha got the two little ones bathed and ready for bed. After getting herself showered she came out of the bathroom and noticed that things weren't as they should be. There by the front door, were three suitcases. Tanisha's mother just stood by the front door with her arms crossed and refused to look at her daughter. "Mom, what's the deal?" Tanisha asked. Her father walked into the room and said, "She's unhappy that you're leaving."

Tanisha had no idea what he was talking about. Her father explained that they knew that she was pregnant again and he decided that she was no longer welcomed in their home. They did not have enough money or energy to support another one of her "messes."

Tanisha was in shock. It was snowing outside. This couldn't really be happening. How could they put her out in the middle of the night? Without discussion, they did. Her father was so mad that he wouldn't even give her time to get dressed or take the suitcases that had been packed. He placed Anneka in Tanisha's arms and then placed JaeTee out the front door and onto the porch. The porch light was turned off and Tanisha and her children were left alone, standing in the dark in their pajamas.

After Tanisha calmed down, she remembered the toll-free number that she had called the prior week. This poor girl was seven months pregnant and now frantically looking for a payphone. She carried Anneka and held JaeTee's hand as they headed toward the Circle K around the corner. Because she was back in Virginia it was extremely late when she called us at 8:00p.m. California time.

We put the Valentine party on hold and began to orchestrate volunteers, shelter, etc. We couldn't leave them standing in a phone booth in the middle of a snow flurry. Within an hour of receiving Tanisha's call, I was able to locate a local volunteer who took Tanisha and the children some clothing and shoes. We made sure that they got settled into a nice, warm motel and had room service scheduled for their breakfast the following morning. Once these things were accomplished air flight was arranged for all of them.

February 15, 2000

We were about to meet the newest member of the "Cuddle Club." I was in the living room at home when I saw Tanisha come through the front door for the first time. She was so beautiful. She had a great big smile that showed off two big dimples and big brown eyes that seemed to sparkle when she talked. Little JaeTee and Anneka were clinging to Tanisha's side. I gave her a big hug as she came into the living room area. Jonathan, our youngest son immediately gravitated to JaeTee. They went right out back and began to swing on the big old rope that hung on the large oak tree in the middle of our yard.

Tanisha told me that she had chosen the family she wanted for her baby. She had already gone out to lunch with them and had plans to do something special over the weekend. The staff at Project Cuddle and the adoptive family would make sure that she had her needs met for the rest of her pregnancy and help her get started with a new life if this was what she wanted after she delivered.

We got her set up in a shelter for unwed mothers and their children. Things seemed to be going all right for the first couple of weeks.

February 28, 2000

I now know more than ever why we need "The Cuddle House," a home where girls and women in similar situations as Tanisha can stay and receive TLC. Unfortunately, one of the other women in the shelter where we had placed Tanisha chose to practice a little theft. The adoptive mother of Tanisha's baby had come to visit Tanisha. Candice, the adoptive mother, had left her purse in Tanisha's room while they went out on a walk. When Candice said her goodbyes she forgot that she had left her purse back in the room. She had no idea that her credit cards had been taken and would be used all across town that weekend. The thief was seen repeatedly leaving the facility with an empty backpack and returning a few hours later with it full. It wasn't until Candice went to her bank on the following Monday that things all came to light. She went up to the teller to cash a check. When the teller saw the name on the check, she commented how she had just cashed a check from her friend. Candice had not written out any checks to friends. Security was called over immediately and they began to review the tapes from the past hour. There on the bank tape was the young lady who had been Tanisha's roommate. The bank ran a check on her and found out that she was wanted in another state for check forgery. It wasn't long before the police moved in to arrest her at the

84

shelter. This woman had charged almost $1,500 on Candice's credit card. Fortunately, the merchandise was recovered as well as most of the cash from Candice's purse.

After that whole situation Candice chose to have Tanisha and her children live with her family through the rest of the pregnancy. Angel was the newest staff member at that time and I had asked her if she wanted to be in the delivery room to assist with the delivery. Angel was extremely excited about being the coach. We all met one afternoon at my house a few weeks before Tanisha was due. I had the five youngest children in our family and Angel brought along her two as well. The adoptive family had their one son and Tanisha had her two. We basically had our own daycare center with a grand total of ten children. The trampoline was up in our back yard, so we went out back and talked as we watched the children take turns jumping. Emily climbed up onto the mat and Beth handed JaeTee into Emily's arms. She began to gently bounce up and down, so JaeTee could try this new experience. JaeTee giggled while bouncing up and down. He had such a contagious laugh that the other children all began to giggle and laugh as well.

We had a great time that day. Tanisha had really bonded with her adoptive family. They had even picked nicknames for each other. Tanisha spoke of one dream. She couldn't wait until after this baby was born. She wanted a Margarita party after she delivered. Tanisha's adoptive family promised that they would help her put such a party together once the baby came.

April 19, 2000

Within a few weeks, Tanisha would be able to have her party. I got the call as I was returning on the Amtrak train from Chicago where I had filmed "Oprah." Tanisha told me that she was now in labor and if I wanted to see the birth of our 200th baby being born, I had better get to the hospital. Angel picked me up from the train station and we took the hour plus drive to the USC Medical Center. Angel was so excited that she could hardly wait to get there, as shown in her Nascar driving skills. When we arrived at the hospital we both got to go in to see Tanisha. She was progressing well and soon Angel was allowed to hold Tanisha's hand as she was given an epidural. We were all allowed in the room as we waited for the 200th Project Cuddle baby to make it's grand appearance. Angel seemed to be doing just as much pushing as Tanisha was. Brian Janson arrived into this world just before 10:30 that night. Tanisha gave one final push and his shoulders appeared and then she blurted out, "Let his new mother cut the cord! Make sure she's the first one to hold him." This whole evening was exactly how I had hoped it would be. After Candice cut the umbilical cord she was handed this precious little boy. He had a great set of lungs. I had a feeling that this was going to be a very vocal little boy.

Tanisha was so content with this whole thing. She knew that she couldn't keep Brian and she was very happy with the Janson Family. They helped her out with her dilemma and she helped them out with theirs. This was a win-win situation. We took pictures of Candice with her new son and Tanisha with him as well. Here Tanisha just delivered a baby and she looked fantastic. In each photo she looked radiant. The last photo we took was of Angel, Tanisha, Baby Brian and I together.

We got home at around 1 a.m. on Sunday. It was another day off that was very well spent. Angel was still in shock over all that had just happened. She had done an awesome job during this her first delivery and I was very proud of her. She learned quickly and would be able to handle other deliveries on her own in the future.

✧✧ UPDATE ✧✧

Well, Tanisha got her Margarita party. The adoptive family as well as our office staff was invited. Tanisha had no regrets about her choice of a family and calls once in a while to check up on the Janson's new son. Their family is now complete with two little boys whom they rescued through Project Cuddle.

After numerous emotional phone calls, Tanisha's family began to miss her and told her that since she was willing to give the baby up she could come back home. Tanisha is now enrolled in school and is doing well. She is close to getting her teaching degree. Hopefully she will come out for a visit someday. We are very grateful that she still keeps in touch with Project Cuddle.

The Tiny Little Bridge Baby

December 6, 1997

What a day this turned out to be. I was asked to be Grand Marshall for a Holiday Festival along with my friend Austin O'Brien. We were supposed to cut the ribbon for a holiday event that was being held for over three thousand underprivileged children. It was pouring outside and had been all night long. The party planner called to let me know that we were still going ahead with the event. They had erected a giant tent just in case the whether got bad. The party was to take place in the middle of Santa Ana. The weather was so bad that as we drove down Harbor Boulevard we could see that the roads were flooded. Trash cans had been blown off the sidewalks and were floating down this four-lane boulevard. Directly in front of us was a beautiful Porsche that had stalled out and was in water up to the bottom of the doors. I was getting nervous. My friend Pilar came along for the ride and said, "Hey, we're surfing in Santa Ana." Everybody chuckled except me. The water was now coming down fast and furious and we were stuck right in the middle of it. I figured that I should just keep going forward slowly and we'd try to take side streets to get past the major flood areas. I had the children all singing "Jesus Loves Me" as we slowly moved through. It was so weird seeing wakes of water behind us moving out from the van as I looked in the rearview mirror.

Dave drove separately to the event, and because he had a one-ton van conversion, he was much higher up and didn't seem fazed by all the water. Though he left about a half hour after we did, he arrived at the same time as us. He had been feeling ill that day. As I stepped down from the podium after cutting the ceremonial ribbon I went over to my handsome husband. I said, "Hello," as he put his arm around my waist. I asked him, "So do you know what today is?" He thought about it for a minute and then said, "It's Saturday." I smiled up at this sweet man and wished him a happy anniversary. He looked so surprised. I told him not to worry about it I was just glad he came to the event. He then gave me an anniversary kiss.

Two days after our anniversary, Dave was still not feeling well. He went to the emergency room because he was having so much pain in his upper stomach area. He was there for almost four hours. When he returned home, they gave him the diagnosis of Hepatitis A. We had to totally rearrange our lives. I began sleeping in the living room, on the sofa. At least I would try to do everything in my power to avoid getting it if that anniversary kiss hadn't gotten me. Dave was so sick that he was barely able to work. He has his own business in our home. He would do as much work as he could and then go back to bed. My daughter Lani ended up helping him out a lot. Everyone had to keep his or her hands clean and avoid Dave as much as possible. Dave was put on a very strict diet. He was not allowed proteins, as they would attack the liver. He was miserable.

January 6, 1998

It was my birthday and I felt awful. I couldn't even dress myself because I was so weak. My heart condition put me in even a tougher spot as I knew that I had contracted Hepatitis A. As a formality, I had to go to a specialist and have blood work done in order to verify it. These results would then be reported to the Health Department. My fever had been up to 105 the night before. Poor Dave was feeling better, but still not in very good shape. We didn't want anyone else to take me for fear that they might contract this thing as well. So, Dave and I went down for my appointment and I was told right there on the spot that I tested positive.

What a way to celebrate one's birthday! The moment I suspected I might have this disease, I began to avoid proteins completely. I didn't want to suffer like Dave had. I was now on complete bed rest for the next three to four months. We couldn't be
near the children or touch anything that they might come in contact
with. I wasn't able to cook for the children, touch things they
might touch, or hug and kiss them. It was so difficult.

No one could come near us. I called to our church, Rock Harbor, and asked if there was any way that the members of the congregation could help with food. Though the church had only been
together for a little over three months, they made a plea on Sunday,
and we were blessed with dinners for the next month and a half. It
was rather interesting. No one would come in, and those delivering
food would usually drop it at the door and run. It was like having
the plague. They brought everything in disposable containers.
Even though all this was going on, it didn't stop the crisis line from
ringing.

My assistant gave her notice, because she was in the midst of
waiting to find out if she was pregnant. This was something that
she and her husband had dreamed of for a long time, and the last
thing they wanted to do was risk her health. The last thing she did
for the charity was to go and film an episode of "Geraldo" for us.
She then had her husband drop everything off at the front door. I
knew she had to do this, but it sure left me in a quandary.

The first few weeks were a total blur. I lay on our sofa in the
living room, unable to climb the stairs. The children would come
in and stand at the far end of the room. I couldn't help them with
their homework or go to parent-teacher conferences. The children
seemed to understand, but it was hard on them.

January 13, 1998

It was 6:45a.m. and the crisis lines began to ring off the hook.
The timing couldn't have been worse. They had rerun an episode
of "Leeza" that we had taped over six months before. Dave and I
each grabbed a phone and I yelled for my daughters, Lani and

91

Elizabeth, to grab a line as well. The lines rang until almost eight o'clock that night. Leeza only gave us about one minute of air time and didn't allow us to tell any frightened woman or girl how we could help, so all the calls we were getting were from people who wanted to get involved as volunteers. It was all I could do just to lie there and write down each address as they called in. When I was feeling a bit better I would fax someone the list of people and they could send out volunteer information packets. There were over 360 phone calls that came in that day. It was going to be a tough few months ahead. We didn't have any more interviews that we were scheduling, so things should be reasonably slow...I thought.

January 19, 1998

NOT!!! I couldn't believe it; they reran an old episode of "Geraldo." This time I got a lot of calls from girls needing help. I still was very weak, but at least my fever was down, so I was really able to concentrate in order to help each girl. Because I was still contagious, I couldn't meet them directly, so I called upon the volunteers in each area where girls and women in crisis were calling. We were able to help with cases in Arizona, Texas, North Carolina, Georgia and more during this time. I ended up rescuing 24 babies and their mothers from abandonment.

April 6, 1998

No more quarantine! No one else in the family contracted it and we were finally able to get back to business as usual. Within a month's time we had two very pregnant girls and women living with us. The first was a young woman by the name of Alexa. She came to us on April 5th and had no prenatal care. We got an appointment for her on the 8th of the month. Her parents had no idea that she was about to delivery a baby. She didn't plan on telling them. She was a very strong Christian who messed up one night. She led the music at church on Sunday morning and evenings. She was having a hard time forgiving herself for this mistake.

The other young woman called the crisis line from a pay phone. We met at a local Coco's on Harbor Blvd. I learned that Rosa happened to love reading anything she could get her hands on. She had found a used copy of the local newspaper on a chair at the local donut shop. In this particular issue there was an article about Project Cuddle. She had been living on her own since the age of fifteen. Her father had abused her until she just couldn't take it any longer. She had befriended a couple of students at school. Their names were Drew and Carlos. Rosa moved in with Carlos' parents. She actually lived in the garage. She, Drew and Carlos spent all their free time together. These living arrangements lasted for a couple of months, until she figured out that Carlos' parents were dealing drugs. She was scared of getting into trouble if they got caught, so she left. Drew had left his parent's house almost three months prior because of some legal problems he had run into. Drew's parents had no idea where he was and he wanted to keep it that way.

Rosa followed Drew to "his place." This ended up being a bridge next to the 405 freeway on-ramp. There was a mattress, shelter from the bridge overhead, a lot of privacy and most importantly...freedom. Over the months that followed, Rosa dropped out of school and learned how to survive by begging for money at the local market parking lot. She got tired of that after awhile, and tried doing phone sales for a change. She would alternate depending on the weather.

Once they actually took off from their little humble abode and hopped a freight train for a vacation. They headed up the California coast and then continued north into Oregon. They stopped in at a logging company and Rosa cooked a few meals while Carlos did some logging. He always asked for cash at the end of each shift. He didn't want his social security card showing up on any records. When they were traveling, they would glean the fruit and vegetable fields. They would locate dairies near the tracks and wait until it was dark to sneak in and milk the cows. They were gone for an entire month at that time.

Rosa and Drew had grown to love each other; they were still in hiding, but happy. Rosa was now eighteen years old and she was about to have a baby. She had no medical insurance and was afraid to apply because she was with Drew. Anything that showed her name would also pop up with his name and then all the warrants would appear. They couldn't afford that. Drew had told Rosa that he was in trouble because of a small accident. She didn't know all the details, but she trusted him. She wouldn't find out until this baby was born what had happened.

Rosa had calculated when she was due and she knew that it should be in the next week or so and Drew insisted that she seek shelter. It had been raining off and on for the past few days, and more rain was on the way. He would stay under the bridge and come and visit her when he got a chance. Rosa and Drew had talked things over and they agreed that they weren't going to keep this baby, but they didn't know what to do with it. They couldn't take a chance on letting anyone discover where they were. They had talked about using fake names or delivering under the bridge and then dropping it off near a school or a hospital.

I talked with both Rosa and Drew about their different options. They decided to look at the photo albums we had that contained families wanting to adopt. They narrowed it down to three families that they wanted to speak with. One was registered with a private adoption agency in Chicago, Illinois. They had two children already but wanted a third. The second was a couple working with an attorney in Santa Monica, California. They didn't have any children and had been waiting for over four years to become parents. The third couple was living in Monterey, California, and had already adopted one child. They had their own ranch and raised horses.

April 7, 1998

Rosa spoke to all three families and had narrowed it down to two. She wanted to meet with the second couple and the third. We arranged for this to take place within the next few days. Even though we had not been successfully able to get Rosa to see the doctors yet, both couples were willing to meet with Rosa and Drew anyway.

94

The first family to come over was the Baxters. They were the couple from Monterey. They brought their little girl Danielle with them. She was very well-behaved for a three year old. They took both Rosa and Drew out to dinner to a little place called Calentinos. Danielle loved the homemade pizza and slowly pulled the cheese and olives off the top as she quietly ate. Rosa loved the minestrone soup that Mr. Calentino prepares fresh each morning. She enjoyed it with a piece of garlic bread. The couples shared their hopes, dreams and philosophies. Though Rosa and Drew thought the Baxters were very nice, she didn't feel anything special. She hoped that she would develop a special feeling when she met with the right family.

The second family to meet with Rosa and Drew were the Gilmores. They arrived almost half an hour late, which they felt so bad about. There had been a traffic accident on the 405 freeway while they were on the way down from Santa Monica. They apologized to both Rosa and Drew over and over for their tardiness. They ended up deciding to spend time playing a game of Risk instead of going out to a restaurant. Pizza was soon delivered and they spent the next four hours playing Risk, sharing their pasts and dreams of building a future. This was the family that both Drew and Rosa wanted to have raise their baby. They would begin the paperwork the following morning. There wasn't any time to waste.

April 9, 1998

What an eventful day it was! We were able to get an appointment for Rosa to meet with the ASP (Adoption Service Provider). Since she had to meet with her twice before she would be able to sign over the baby for adoption, we were glad that we could get this started so fast. After a two-hour appointment we took both Rosa and Drew out to Mimi's Café. Boy, could that girl eat! The table was full of dishes by the time we finished eating. We went to meet with the Gilmore's attorney to get paperwork in order for the hospital. The attorney they had retained, Steven Lazarus, was wonderful. He was a young man in his mid-thirties and a father of one with twins on the way. He was very patient with Drew as he struggled to fill out the paper work. Drew had never completed school.

He had always been challenged with reading and eventually gave up on school altogether in the 11th grade. Steven helped explain the final portion of the paperwork and gave him time to finish signing at the designated spots. Rosa and Drew were both still very sure that this was what they wanted to do.

April 10, 1998

I was able to get an appointment for Rosa at the same time as I was taking Alexa to the obstetrician. They both entered the building and walked into the doctor's office. Alexa led Rosa over to the receptionist's area and signed in. Rosa followed suit. Each took her turn seeing the obstetrician. Alexa was told that her due date was May 1, 1998. This meant that we had less than a month to help Alexa figure out what she wanted to do. She was a very nurturing person and would probably make a good mother. She was also very smart and had high hopes of completing college. I wouldn't be surprised if Alexa ended up asking for us to help tell her parents and then keep her baby. Only time would tell.

Rosa was told that she was dilated to two and would probably deliver in the next few days. Rosa was really startled by this. She wasn't prepared. She began to panic. "I'm not ready...wait, I need more time," she proclaimed. The doctor chuckled as he listened to her. I reassured Rosa that we would help her get everything done and this would all work out just fine. I told her, "Look at it this way, you're almost done. No more getting up in the middle of the night to go to the bathroom, no more heartburn." She smiled and realized that it was true. She was on the home stretch and it could be a lot worse. I took Rosa back home. She was really depressed and scared. She could only think of seeing Drew. I encouraged her to call the Gilmore's home and let them know how her doctor appointment went. They weren't home so she left a message. I think it would have cheered her up if she could have had a chance to talk with them directly. It had started to rain really hard outside; there was a lot of thunder and lightening. She refused to eat dinner that night. As she went to bed, I promised that I would take her the following morning to see Drew.

96

April 11, 1998

I woke up in the morning and went downstairs to wake Rosa up for the day. To my surprise she wasn't in her room. I looked throughout the house and couldn't find her anywhere. I gently woke Alexa up and asked her if she had any idea where Rosa could be. She had no idea. All she knew was that Rosa really missed Drew. Alexa figured she was back under the bridge with Drew. I couldn't believe that she could be out there in the pouring rain and close to delivering a baby.

I quickly got dressed and headed out in the Cuddle Van to try and find her. It only took me five minutes to get to the edge of the freeway where I parked. Then I had to walk in under the bridge. There, in the far corner lying on a dirty old queen size mattress was Rosa. Drew was snuggled up next to Rosa and sound asleep. Rosa wasn't asleep. She was just lying there, staring into space. As I approached Rosa I whispered, "Are you all right?"

Rosa turned her head toward me and looked into my eyes. "I'm so scared," she sobbed. I went over to her side and sat down on the filthy ground next to her. I reached my arm out and placed my hand on her forehead. She was shaking as I stroked her hair. I tried to reassure her that everything was going to be just fine. We should all go back to my house and sit by the nice warm fire in front of the fireplace. Lani could make the hot cocoa and Beth could pop some popcorn.

Drew began to wake up as we continued talking. I was almost certain that Rosa was having contractions every five minutes or so. I took my coat off and wrapped it around Rosa when she sat up. "Look," I said, "let's go to my place." I found myself being a cheerleader for the cause. It took me about fifteen minutes, three contractions and a half-inch of rain, but we got Rosa to leave the security of her bridge.

I knew we were about to go to the hospital, but did not want to spook Rosa. We stopped at my house and checked in on the children. Though Rosa had only been around for a short time, she had really grown attached to my son Tyler. He had been busy creating a new costume while we were out in the pouring rain. As we came into the living room Tyler made his way over to Rosa. "Hey Rosa." Tyler was wearing bright yellow Playtex rubber gloves on his feet. "Ya like it? I'm a duck." Rosa began giggling and then grabbed her stomach. Another contraction. This one was stronger than the last.

I helped get Rosa over to a chair. Drew came to her side and asked if he could come along and help take her to the hospital. He tried to reassure her that it was time and everything would be fine. The contractions were strong enough now that she was willing to go. She actually asked me to call the Gilmore family as we began packing her bag. (It's funny, but about 99 percent of the girls we work with never have a bag packed for the hospital, even after they make a decision to have the baby in the hospital.)

We got Rosa to the hospital and the Gilmores arrived within an hour. They were very nervous. Rosa asked for them to come into the labor room once she was settled in. She told them how much she appreciated what they were doing for Drew and her. She felt that there would never be a way for her to repay them. They tried to help her understand that they had the utmost respect for her and would love her forever for the precious gift she was giving them.

It looked as though it was going to be at least five or six more hours before the baby was ready to make it's entrance into the world. The Gilmores stepped out and went down to the cafeteria for a bite to eat. While they were gone all heck broke loose. The baby's heart rate began to drop drastically. There was no time to wait. The doctors had to gown up and rush Rosa in for an emergency C-section. I was allowed to gown up and go in too. Drew knew that he would have passed out at the first sight of blood so he was very content to let me stand by Rosa's side.

Rosa had been given some medication so she wasn't nearly as frightened as she would have been. Her vitals were fine as we headed for the operating room. The baby's were not. It didn't look good. The doctor thought that the cord might be wrapped around its neck. We only had a few steps to go from the labor room to the operating room. This was definitely a good thing.

The operating room was all ready and waiting for Rosa. They wheeled her in and she lifted herself from the gurney to the operating table. The anesthesiologist spoke briefly with Rosa and let her know that he would be giving her just enough medication to keep her awake but comfortable. I talked with her as they began the procedure. I told her that the Gilmores would be waiting outside the operating room doors.

The monitor was showing that the baby's heart rate was drastically low now. The doctors began the operation and quickly got to the baby. They found the umbilical cord was wrapped twice around the baby's neck. I watched as he loosened the cord and removed it. Now he could safely remove the baby from what was home for the past nine months. Rosa was stable and now it looked as though the baby would be fine. The doctor announced that we had a little boy. I could see his limp, blue little body being lifted over to the waiting pediatric nurse. Her hand held a large green towel that soon enveloped his tiny body. The surgeon clamped and then cut the umbilical cord. The baby was quickly examined and suctioned. The room was quiet as the pediatrician examined the baby. A respiratory therapist administered oxygen and the baby was finally heard crying.

We all breathed a sigh of relief. Rosa had no idea that there had been any problem and that was the way I planned on keeping it. She did not even seem to notice his little cry. Rosa finally asked me if everything was all right. I told her that it was a boy and he was breathing now and beginning to turn pink. She smiled a bit and then drifted off as she was sutured up.

Outside the operating room doors stood Pamela and Bradford Gilmore. They would not be sleeping through nights for some time to come. The double doors opened and I was the lucky one that got to ask, "Hey Mommy and Daddy, would you like to see your new son?" They were so cute. Pamela began to cry as she approached her son. Bradford proudly stood behind his wife with a hand on each of her shoulders. Family and friends were there to snap shots of this special moment; Tyler even wore a special outfit for this day's event. He had found an old pair of hospital scrubs that were way too big, but stayed on with the help of a telephone cord that normally was used to connect the headpiece to the main body of the phone.

As the nurse who was holding the baby, and I headed toward the NICU nursery, Pamela and Bradford followed behind. Their son was doing much better now. He was breathing on his own, but the respiratory therapist followed alongside just in case the baby began to have problems. As we stood outside the NICU doors, I asked Pamela and Bradford if they had chosen a name yet. "Yes, we decided that since Steven had helped us so much with making this adoption possible, we were going to name it after him. His name is Steven Michael Gilmore." They both smiled at the baby and then each other before disappearing into the scrub room area to prepare to enter the NICU. Soon they would be holding their son in their arms.

✧✧ UPDATE ✧✧

Pamela and Bradford have adjusted beautifully to being parents. Their son, rescue baby #14, went from five pounds at birth to being a hefty little two-year old. He is on target with his milestones and loves to socialize. He loves giving kisses and catching bugs. I thought this was quite a combination.

Drew and Rosa have moved on. Drew never told Rosa why he was hiding from the law, but one day the local authorities eventually took Drew away. Rosa found out that Drew had been in an accident when he was seventeen. The problem was that it was hit and run. Drew was arrested and served two years and is now on probation. Rosa finished school while Drew was away and now works as a cosmetologist in our local neighborhood. She says that she is now going to support Drew while he goes back to school and gets his GED. They are planning on getting married this coming summer and we will be active participants in the ceremony.

Hurricane Bonnie

August 19, 1998

When Mandy called our crisis line for the first time, she was really down. She was from Wilmington, North Carolina. She told me that she was sure that she was pregnant, but had no idea what to do. She had lost custody of her three-year-old son because she was using drugs. He was now in foster care and was going to be adopted by the family that had cared for him since he was born. Yes, she was still using, but was trying to stay clean. She would go a couple of days without using anything, and then the withdrawals would get so bad that she would go out and use again.

She hadn't had any prenatal care, and had no idea where she could go. We were able to locate a place for her to be seen that was familiar with caring for those who were drug abusers. They were able to place her on a methadone program and monitor her through-out the rest of her pregnancy.

Mandy wasn't sure what she wanted to do in regards to the baby she was carrying. She was thinking about keeping it and yet she knew that as long as she was using drugs, it would be taken away from her at birth and put into foster care. She had thought about adoption, but couldn't handle the thought of giving it up to some stranger, never to be seen again.

I told her not to worry about it right now. She had time to think it all over. First and most importantly, we needed to get her in for her first prenatal visit. She called me back after the visit and we took the next step towards a solution for Mandy and her baby.

August 22, 1998

Mandy called me early that morning. She was anxious to let us know that she had gotten to the clinic. She told me that she was very confused. She was excited about starting on the methadone program, but she was upset because she found out that she was carrying twins. They gave her a due date of December 23, 1998, but because they were twins, they would probably come early. The lab had taken blood and was checking her for STDs (sexually transmitted diseases), but those results wouldn't be back for a few days.

With this new revelation, Mandy was seriously considering finding a family to adopt her babies. She knew that she could barely take care of herself, let alone care for two others. She didn't know the father of the babies. It had been a one-night stand and she only remembered that he told her his first name was Mike. The attorney she would choose would take that information and make sure that Mike's rights were terminated so that the couple adopting the baby would have the security of knowing that these babies were truly theirs.

August 24, 1998

Bad news, Mandy tested positive for syphilis. She immediately started treatment and stuck to her methadone program. Between 40 to 70 percent of such pregnancies will yield a syphilis-infected infant.[2] These babies were not getting the easiest start, but hopefully we would be able to locate some wonderful families that Mandy would be willing to speak with. She seemed to be looking for a family that was willing to have an open adoption. She wanted photos once a year and a letter telling about their growth. She gave me some specifics that she felt were important in a family.

Though we had Mandy under a doctor's care, she wasn't out of the woods. We had a new problem coming our way. Hurricane Bonnie had just formed off the Atlantic Coast. Mandy had mentioned it in passing, but she figured it would go further up the coast and miss her completely.

August 25, 1998

Hurricane Bonnie was getting frighteningly close to land. I called to check in on Mandy. She told me that she had been helping to board up the windows and purchased candles and a lantern in case the power went out. She had some extra canned goods that she had collected and boxed up. I knew that there was nothing I could do to help her since I was all the way out in California, but I was definitely a nervous wreck for the next few days.

Mandy didn't seem very concerned. She'd been through enough storms to know what was coming. There was the bust with Hurricane Felix in 1995 and then Hurricane Bertha in 1996. Both those years she had panicked and prepared; then the hurricanes never touched down in their area. Once she rode through one, a little one, just fine and felt confident that this was going to be the same. She went to the clinic and got the prescription for the medication needed to help her with the STD. I was to call her back in the morning and check up on her.

August 26, 1998

Hurricane Bonnie edged into North Carolina's southern coastline near Wilmington. Bonnie was the first major hurricane (Category 3) of the 1998 season, and the winds and flooding rains began to damage buildings and the power was cut off to nearly a half-million people by the end of the night. The storm was nearly 400 miles wide and it stalled near Wilmington for an hour after its "eye" crossed land at Cape Fear at 5 p.m.[1]

I tried calling Bonnie all day long. The lines were down and we had no way of getting in touch with her. She would have to contact us. Now we could only sit back and wait until she contacted us. Fortunately, there was plenty to keep me busy. I transferred the crisis line to my cell phone and headed toward the YMCA for the children's swimming lessons. I was glad to be able to keep myself busy. As I was driving, Jonathon asked me a very serious question. He asked, "Mom, how do they make bologna? Does it grow on trees?" Now that was probably the only laugh I was going to be

103

able to muster up for the day, at least until we heard from Mandy.

The day wore into night and I still couldn't get through to her. The news stations were reporting that at least two people had been killed because of the hurricane. I finally went to bed knowing that a call could possibly come in the middle of the night and I'd think a lot clearer if I had a little rest.

August 27, 1998

I awoke early that morning and located the piece of paper with Mandy's phone number on it. The phone lines were still down. I went downstairs and checked the weather report. There were now three deaths that had been caused by this hurricane. There had been a lot of flooding and extensive damage to buildings throughout the town.

Finally at 9:00 p.m., I got a call from her. She told me that she was all right, but had been through a lot. Mandy's apartment suffered a lot of damage. The tree from the house next door fell down onto her apartment. It came partially through the roof and destroyed her living room. Fortunately she was taking a nap at the time it fell, so she wasn't hurt, but it sure woke her up in a hurry.

At least two inches of rain poured into her living room. She ended up with debris from neighboring homes and yards on top of her water-soaked carpet. She told me that airborne missiles came flying in at over 70 miles an hour. She shut herself in the bedroom for fear of being hit by objects that might be entering the building. She said, "I was so scared that I pushed my dresser up against the door! I didn't know what else to do. The phones were down so I couldn't even call for help."

After the hurricane passed, the landlord came over to check on Mandy. They helped her get over to the Red Cross Emergency Relief Center. It had been set up at a school in the next town. She would be staying there for the next few weeks until they were able to get her apartment in order. Over the next month we heard from Mandy whenever she got a free moment. She was still going to the clinic for all her medication and check-ups. All the regular telephone lines remained down for quite a while. She had to look for pay phones in order to call our toll-free crisis line. That wasn't always easy. Even when she did find one, there might be ten to twenty people in line ahead of her. The National Guard sent troops out to protect the damaged properties against vandalism.

November 22, 1998

She was finally able to get back into her place and it looked great. She got new carpet and drapes and they provided her with a brand new sofa set that was better than the one she had before. Because she was having premature contractions, Mandy had been placed on complete bed rest. She was now certain that she wanted to give the babies a better chance at life than she was able to give them. She had not told her parents about this pregnancy and since they lived a couple of hours away, she decided to keep it from them completely. She was very specific about the family she wanted. She was looking for a family that would be willing to stay in touch with her through letters and photos. She didn't care what state they lived in, as long as they were willing to stay in touch. The other key thing that Mandy was looking for in a family was that they were vegetarians. This was something Mandy was emphatic about.

This was not an easy task to accomplish. We checked through all the families that had submitted "birth mother letters" and none of them fit this criterion at all. We put feelers out to attorneys and agencies trying to locate families that Mandy could speak with. We didn't have much time left, so there was a lot of praying going on.

November 26, 1998
Thanksgiving Day

We found two families for Mandy to consider. She spoke with both of them on the phone and had no doubt as to which was the right one for her children. They understood that these were going to be special little babies and that they may have some medical needs that were above and beyond the normal situation. The families didn't care. They wanted to be parents at any cost. The family she ended up choosing told me, "Adoption should be about the children; we should adopt because a child needs us. It shouldn't be about shopping for the perfect child to fill our dreams and wishes. It's about what we can do for a child." (I liked what they had to say).

What a wonderful Thanksgiving it was. Mandy called to tell me that she was in labor and the doctors were going to go ahead with the C-section in the next few hours. The Bergen family was on their way to the hospital. They only had a two-hour flight, so they would probably get there before the babies were born. Mandy was nervous, but anxious to get this all over with.

Donna and Mark Bergen stood outside the operating room waiting for the news of their new children. Donna had been through three miscarriages in the past four years. She and Mark had been married for almost ten years and had tried to have children for the past five years. The last pregnancy was the last straw. She carried the baby full term and though everything seemed fine throughout the entire nine months, the baby stopped moving. When Donna went in to have a stress test done, they couldn't find the baby's heartbeat. Three days before her due date, the baby's heart just stopped beating.

Finally, the doors to the operating room opened. Dr. Cline walked out and pulled his mask down as he walked toward the anxious couple. "Congratulations Mr. and Mrs. Bergen. You are the proud parents of a little boy and a little girl." They grabbed each other and hugged. Donna wept as she asked the doctor, "Can we see them? How is Mandy?" The doctor smiled and told them that they could go to the nursery and see the babies.

As the new parents approached the nursery window, Mark mouthed Mandy's last name to the nurse. She told them that they would be down in a minute. Once the two incubators arrived, Mark and Donna were allowed to gown up and go in to watch as their babies were weighed, measured and then placed under warming lamps. Katherine Grace weighed in at 4 pounds 3 ounces and was 17 inches long. David Michael weighed in at a hefty 5 pounds even and was 17 ½ inches long. Both rescue babies #129 and #130 were breathing room air and had good color.

Mandy slept through the night and did very well at taking her first walk after the C-section. She would meet with the hospital social worker in the morning and then the Bergen's attorney. I was sure that she would be fine, but wished so much that I could be there in person for her.

November 30, 1998

The day finally came for Katherine and David to travel with their new parents to the state where they would now live. They said their goodbyes to Mandy and she gently gave each baby a kiss on the forehead. She looked at David and Katherine and then up at Mark and Donna. "Go, before I start to cry. Take your little babies and go have a good life." She embraced Donna as she held David and then Mark as he held Katherine. This was the last they would see of her for a while. Bottles, diapers, car seats and babies were soon relocated to their new home. A big sign was taped to the garage door. It read, "Welcome home Davie & Katie." Donna was finally realizing that this was real. She was really the mother of two babies and wife to a wonderful husband. Her life was now complete.

✧✧ UPDATE ✧✧

The Bergen family is doing just fine. The babies are tested every six months for STD's and have remained clean. They have decided that they will someday adopt again and are certain that they will offer to adopt special needs children.

Mandy has cleaned up her life. She is now going to a trade school and will soon graduate as a cashier. She loves what she is doing and realizes that the babies are much better off where they are. She gets letters and pictures every six months. Mandy will see the twins for the first time since she kissed them goodbye in the hospital. This will take place on their third birthday.

Chapter Five

Fearful of the System

Introduction

Approximately fifty percent of all the girls and women who come to Project Cuddle for assistance were either in foster care or adopted. For the most part, they are "Fearful of 'the System'." I found a great compassion for what these women went through in their lives and realized that it was extremely hard for them to reach out because they were afraid of being "swallowed up."

The Little Princess

August 1, 1999

The crisis line rang and I picked it up just as I did daily. It was a young lady by the name of Jackie. She had heard about Project Cuddle from a girlfriend, Lucy. Lucy had heard a radio program on KHPY radio. Both girls had been in foster care together when they were young. Jackie had become a foster child at the age of three. She couldn't remember much about her birth family now that she was eighteen years old, but she did remember what she had been told about her past and it wasn't pretty.

She had been told that her father would get angry when she was small and often threaten her mother with torturing the children in front of her. It was his way of keeping control over his wife and getting back at her for things she had done wrong. She hated it when he went after the children. She tried to be a good wife and get dinner on the table when he would arrive home each evening, but with four children five-years-old and under, it wasn't always possible. She honestly went out of her way to try and keep him happy. She knew that she or her kids would suffer if he wasn't respected. One particular day had been extremely rough. The children had been extremely fussy and one had a cold. She just couldn't seem to get ahead with anything. She seemed to have an extra large amount of laundry to do and put an extra amount of concentration into catching up on it. She forgot to take something out of the freezer for dinner that evening. When her husband got in that evening, he saw that dinner wasn't ready and decided that she needed to be punished for this.

He decided that he would grab the nearest child and hang it out the window of their second story apartment. He really wanted to scare her good this time. He grabbed little Jackie by the arm and said, "Come here ya little brat, let's teach your mother a lesson." He then walked over to the window and opened it, as he began to lift Jackie up by one arm he grabbed one of her legs as well. Jackie's mother screamed and yelled, "No John! Don't do that. This isn't funny. Just put her back down and I'll get your damn dinner!" "Now you've done it!" John shouted. "You know better than to swear in my house!" He took the upside down child by both legs and hung her outside the window. Little Jackie screamed as her father swung her back and forth over the concrete. "Stop it John!" were the last words that Jackie would hear before she was dropped to the pavement below.

Jackie lay unconscious. One of the neighbors who lived across the street had heard Jackie's screams and looked out the window just before John let go. She ran out of her apartment and knelt down next to Jackie's tiny body. There in front of her, Jackie's tiny body began to contract with a seizure. The terrified woman cried out for help. Within minutes sirens could be heard. Paramedics took over in trying to help Jackie the minute they arrived.

The police rushed up the flight of stairs and stormed into the Clark's apartment. When John saw the gun pointed at him, he decided to give up without a fight. The second officer who arrived on the scene noticed some drug paraphernalia that was laying on the coffee table. He called for social services to come and assist in taking custody of the rest of the children who were in the house. He knew he would now need to take their mother in as well as their father. The house was a mess. There were soiled diapers in corners of the room and fast food wrappers stuffed under the edges of the stain-soiled sofa. As the officers collected the three other children, the siren could be heard as it finally took off with Jackie. It had taken them fifteen minutes to stabilize her broken body. She was now on her way to the local trauma center. Her siblings would now be taken to the doctor at the same facility and checked out to make sure they didn't have any breaks or bruises. The officers all knew that the children might not ever see Jackie or each other

112

again. This was definitely the toughest part of the officer's job.

Over the next few weeks, Jackie fought to stay alive. After they got her seizures stabilized, and set her left arm, they were able to get her into a foster home for the medically fragile. She stayed there for the next three months and was then moved into a regular foster home. The best part about this move was the fact that Jackie was finally able to be with her siblings again. This would be a year filled with wonderful memories for all four of them.

Over the next several years, life changed for the worse. Jackie's parents would try minimally to follow the service plan that the court ordered them to complete. They had been ordered to take parenting classes, attend NA meetings and hold legal employment. If they were able to complete these requirements and get stable housing, they just might become a family again. Eventually, their rights were terminated and the children were put up for adoption. The problem was that no one wanted the entire set of children. Jackie was the last one to be adopted. The family that was chosen for her wasn't, shall we say, "the dream family" of every child. For example, the parents would go on vacation but never take her. They would leave her behind with a baby sitter. She lived within two hours of Disneyland, but had never gone there.

Now, we had a very frightened teen who had just turned eighteen and wanted to get out of her current living situation. She said, "My adoptive father and I fight all the time. He drinks a lot and we just don't get along." When I asked her about the fighting, she told me that she would actually get into physical fights with this guy. I was worried for her safety, especially now that she was pregnant.

Her adoptive parents knew that she was pregnant and they had unfortunately reacted as so many parents do. She had been called a "slut," a "whore," and a "tramp." She was commanded to give the baby up through the religious sect that her adoptive mother was very heavily involved with. This wasn't at all what Jackie wanted for her baby. She was so depressed by this that she actually tried to commit suicide during the pregnancy. Fortunately, her former foster sister had heard about Project Cuddle and now would be able to get Jackie the help she needed.

When I spoke to her I learned a lot about her. I learned more about what she wanted for herself in the future and what she wanted for the baby. She told me that she had always wanted to travel and in fact had just joined the army with the hopes of traveling when she found out she was pregnant. This messed up everything. She decided that she wanted a family that would travel.

When I last spoke with Jackie, she thought that she would try and face her family by herself and let them know that she didn't want anything to do with the religious organization that they were pushing her to work with. The family's religious beliefs had been so pushed on Jackie that she had turned the other direction. The family even moved out into the middle of the desert so that Jackie wouldn't have any possible way of being around the "evil forces" of the general population of sinners.

August 3, 1999

Two days after my initial conversation with Jackie, I got another call from her. "I want you to come down and meet with me," she said. I could tell that she was upset. I asked her what was wrong and she told me that she had another fight with her adoptive father. She wanted to get out of the house, but was so afraid of what lay beyond her tiny town called Cathedral City. I told her that I would come down and meet with her. She could then decide what she wanted to do.

I brought along a volunteer so that I wouldn't be alone if the conversation was uncomfortable or in case I got a crisis call on the cell phone while I was with her. Jackie gave me her address and directions on how to get to her. I was instructed to call from my cell phone when I was about five minutes away from her house. If she told me she couldn't go anywhere because of a headache, that meant that her mother hadn't left for work yet. When I tried to place the call, I couldn't get through. Her place was so far out from the main city that I couldn't get any phone service. I had to drive back about five miles in order to get the call to go through. When

114

she picked up the phone she told me that it was safe to come up. I had left the "Cuddle Van" at home so that no neighbor would see the signs on the sides of the van and then tell Jackie's mother who had picked her up. It would be up to Jackie as to whether or not she told her family where she had gone. I drove on up the hill and headed toward Jackie's house. The volunteer, Clarissa was driving her van that day. She was rather nervous. This was the first time that she had helped me on a case where we had to meet a girl confidentially. She pulled the van up to the front of Jackie's house. I called on the cell phone to let Jackie know we were there. Of course, I couldn't get through, but had instinctively dialed anyway.

Clarissa and I went up to the front door. She said, "Oh my gosh...I can't believe we're doing this." A beautiful young lady answered the door. I asked, "Jackie, are you Jackie?" "Yes, I am," she said as she looked into my eyes with her beautiful green ones. She had the cutest little turned up nose, and her smile revealed the cutest tiny teeth. "Come in," she said. We entered into the living room. The house was simple. It needed a good cleaning, and from what I had gathered, it was always up to Jackie to do that. She had been too worn down to do as much as this house needed.

We waited as Jackie picked up her purse and then we all headed back to the van. It was another 20 minutes just to get back to the local restaurants. I asked Jackie what kind of food she was craving and she directed Clarissa to the "Home Town Buffet." They had a little bit of everything there. This was the first time that I had ever been to one. It was every pregnant woman's dream. Jackie ate enough for two people, possibly three, that day.

By the time we finished our meal, Jackie told me that she had changed her mind. She wanted to come back to Orange County with us and start her life all over again. She was so scared because she felt that Orange County was so far away. She had never been out of the city limits since being adopted. She told me that it seemed as though she was going to a foreign country. She asked Clarissa to drive her back to the house so she could pick up everything. I didn't want to say anything, but I was worried that her mother might show up while we were there. Jackie reassured us that it would not be a problem. My heart was pounding as we approached her street. "Just turn around Clarissa if her mom's car is there. Jackie, you will duck down so she doesn't see you, okay?" They both agreed and we turned the corner. The coast was clear.

We went into Jackie's kitchen and got plastic trash bags so we could fill them with all her belongings. In her bedroom we asked if items were hers and if they should be packed. It was so sad. By the time we finished filling the two trash bags, we had all her belongings. It was as though everything she had in her room was just on loan.

Jackie seemed happier now that she had made her decision. She had basically been held, almost like a hostage, with no car, no license, and completely away from any and all kids her age. In her parents' eyes, she was for the time being safe and not able to get into much trouble. This was definitely not going to make them happy. For the first time since adopting their daughter, they would have no control.

We traveled towards Orange County, and I felt relieved when we got within the county limits. Now we would begin to help Jackie as she grappled with all the decisions that lay ahead. Our main goal was to make sure that she was in charge of her life and each decision she would have to make.

As we neared the corner to my home, I could see little Jonathon riding his tricycle in the front yard. Tyler wasn't far behind him on his scooter. Jonathon kept on riding, but Tyler, in his true "Tigger form," came bouncing over to the van. "Hi, whatcha doin?" he questioned.

As I helped settling her in, I began to learn more about her. She had become pregnant by an older man that was her boss at work. She didn't love him, but felt that if she didn't give in to his desires, she was in jeopardy of losing her job. She finally confronted him when she found out she was pregnant and he let her go. Poor Jackie didn't know what to do. She had followed her parents' requests and had gone through their church in order to please them.

116

When she went to the bishop and told him how unhappy she was, he told her she should, "Ponder and pray about it." In other words, "Sit down, be quiet and do what your parents tell you to do." This had all seemed so hopeless until Jackie called us. Now, she was taking control and seeking out her destiny as well as her baby's.

August 10, 1999

Jackie had decided on a family that not only traveled but also had their own plane. This little baby would see everything that Jackie had missed out on. She actually met Clarissa for the first time the day that we picked her up to relocate and three days later met Clarissa's husband. She told me that she knew instantly that this was the family for her. She loved how Larry carried their two-year-old son, Geoffrey, up on his shoulders. He was such a nurturing father. She became instant friends with Clarissa and wished that the Winslows could have adopted her as well.

August 11, 1999

I took Jackie to her first doctor appointment in Orange County. We met Clarissa there at the office and we all went in together to watch as they did the ultrasound. Clarissa held Jackie's hand as they ran the device over Jackie's large belly. "There, you can see it's going to be a girl," the technician proclaimed. Jackie didn't seemed fazed by it, but Clarissa and I immediately got tears in our eyes. I knew that Clarissa would be thrilled just to have any baby, but her heart truly wanted a little girl that she could dress up and take shopping. Now, her dream was about to come true. The technician passed us both the box of tissue. We would soon meet with the doctor and get a better gauge on when she was due. According to this ultrasound, the baby was due the second week of September. It contradicted the original ultrasound that had been done many months before. That one gave a due date of August 30th. We hoped that the doctor would shed some light on this and Jackie had hoped that the first ultrasound was the right one. She didn't want to carry this baby any longer than necessary.

We met with the doctor. He was a handsome young man. I had

never worked with him before and hoped that he would have an open mind and understand that the girls I work with aren't your typical pregnant girls. He examined Jackie and then told her that she could go for another whole month. This meant that she might not deliver until the end of September. Knowing Jackie as I did, I knew that there was no way she would be able to hold on that long. I pulled the doctor aside and tried to explain to him the fragile state that Jackie was in. Somehow I needed for him to understand how difficult this was for Jackie. I didn't feel as though he got it, and I left the building with a very depressed and still very pregnant young lady.

The doctor that we normally used for these deliveries was in the midst of changing hospitals. The hospital where he normally did his deliveries had closed the doors to its labor and delivery unit. I hoped that he would find a hospital soon (just in case this new doctor didn't work out). This new doctor seemed intelligent, but I did not feel that he respected what Jackie was saying and the concerns she had, but only time would tell.

Clarissa suggested that we stop somewhere for lunch. We went to the local "Olive Garden" and Jackie devoured everything that was put in front of her, including the dessert. It was funny, but most girls who came out to us seemed to be rather small when they first arrived, but within a week they seemed to pop right out. Jackie did just that.

Over the next week, Jackie really got to know Clarissa and Larry. They took her to the movies, shopping and several other outings. We began to schedule meetings with the ASP (Adoption Service Provider) and a meeting with the attorney. With both of those meetings out of the way, we could try to focus on keeping Jackie happy for the next few weeks.

August 20, 1999

Jackie was growing very restless. She had been to the doctor's office and he told her she needed to stay off her feet. This caused some big frustrations for her, as she was very angry that she wouldn't be able to do anything. I went out and purchased a Game Boy so that she would have something to do. We got videos and tried to arrange for people to visit her. One special friend was Linda Campbell. She was a makeup artist for the entertainment industry. She came down and did Jackie's hair and makeup; Jackie felt much better. Though each day was a challenge, we were able to keep her pretty happy over all.

August 21, 1999

Jackie thought she was in labor. She wasn't sure, but she thought her bag of water was leaking. I called the doctor and let him know what was going on. He suggested that I bring her into the emergency room to get checked out. Jackie was scared, but rather excited that this might all be coming to an end. She hoped that this was labor and that she would hand the Winslows her little "problem" before the day was done.

We went up to the labor and delivery unit. They had her fill out some papers and then showed us to a labor room that held four beds. They strapped a fetal heart monitor to Jackie's belly. We heard the fast little beats of her unborn child and Clarissa and Larry's future baby.

For the next hour Jackie was monitored. Unfortunately, it didn't show anything significant as far as contractions. When they told Jackie, she got very quiet. After they left the room, Jackie whispered under her breath, "I hate this stupid baby!"

I told Jackie that I understood that she was frustrated, but we would have to leave for now and hang in there for a few more weeks. Perhaps it could only be a few days if her due date was truly August 30th, but we would just have to take it one day at a time.

I called the Winslows on the cell phone as Jackie and I headed toward home. I wanted to give them a heads-up so that they would be extra sensitive to her emotional state. In turn, Clarissa contacted my family to let them know what was going on. Beth, our ten-year-old knew how much Jackie loved chocolate chip cookies, so she began baking some as we headed towards home. Our son Bejay, who was also ten, went with our oldest daughter Lani to "Blockbuster." Bejay picked out a couple of cassettes for the Game Boy and Lani picked out a couple of videotapes that she thought Jackie would enjoy. By the time we got home, the whole house smelled of warm fresh-baked cookies and the tape was already in the VCR, ready and waiting.

The next few days were rough for everybody. Clarissa got so worried that Jackie was going to change her mind. I wasn't sure where she got this idea, but Clarissa was truly frightened. She gathered the support of her younger sister Sara and they decided to go shopping to try and focus on the fact that they are truly going to be parents. So, as "Nordstrom's" opened their doors Clarissa and her sister walked in. They bought a beautiful, light pink satin bedspread, crib sheets, matching comforter, and bumper pads. Sara bought a beautiful sterling silver rattle for her niece-to-be. Things would work out she told Clarissa and this was her way of showing confidence. Though she too had some doubt, she kept it deep inside her so that her sister would never know.

September 7, 1999

Jackie was at her wit's end. She blurted out, "It's been ten days people! According to my first ultrasound I'm ten days overdue!" I listened as Jackie threatened to go to Tijuana and have the baby taken out. I tried to calm her down. Then I called the doctor that we had been seeing. I explained to him what was going on with Jackie and yet he didn't really grasp how serious this was. He told me that he wanted to hold off for another two weeks. He wasn't about to induce. I couldn't tell this to Jackie. This would definitely send her over the edge.

I knew we had to act quickly because Jackie definitely meant what she said. I believe that when God shuts the front door there's a side window or door left open. I knew I had to figure something out. I remembered the doctor that I normally worked with and hoped that he had located a new hospital that he could work with. I gave him a call and explained the situation. He knew exactly what I was worried about and didn't waste any time getting her in for an appointment. He had just become affiliated with Garden Grove Hospital and many of the nurses that we had previously worked with at the last hospital were working there. I was so relieved. "Forget the other doctor, we are going to the best," I told Jackie. We got an appointment scheduled for the following morning so my only concern was getting her through that evening. She actually came to me and told me that if she had enough money, she would get an abortion today. I suggested that we pack her bag and focus on the fact that she was most likely going to have a baby born in the next 24 hours.

September 8, 1999

That following morning I took Clarissa and a very grumpy Jackie to the doctor. We entered the waiting room and I went on in and spoke with the doctor while Jackie filled out papers. I explained to the doctor the different due dates and ultrasounds. I stood next to her while he measured her belly and listened to the baby's heart rate. Jackie was very much to the point with him. She told him how she wanted this over NOW and she knew that this baby was ten days overdue.

He took into account all the ultrasound photos and her last menstrual cycle as well as her measurements. He asked Jackie, "Would you like to go in this evening or wait until the morning?" She was so surprised. She perked right up and looked up into his eyes. "To the hospital?" she questioned. "Yes, you want to have the baby right?" He smiled. She gleefully stated, "Oh yeah, let's go in today."

We were glad that we had packed her bag. Clarissa drove us over to Garden Grove Hospital. The social worker was already aware of our case and pending arrival. In fact, she was in the lobby when we arrived. She was so pleasant and took us right over to the registration area. Once we got Jackie signed in, we went upstairs and found her room. The room was simple, but clean. After she got into a hospital gown, she climbed into bed and looked pleasantly relaxed. This poor girl had no idea what she was about to go through. She would soon learn what the meaning of labor really was. The doctor came in and explained that he would be giving her something that would help soften the cervix. It was going to take around twelve hours or more to work, but then we would be able to see her progress.

September 9, 1999

I slept sitting up in the chair next to Jackie's bed that night. At around two in the morning as I was sleeping, all of the sudden I felt a slap from the back of Jackie's hand as it hit my upper arm. Boy, was I startled. She quietly looked at me and with tears in her eyes, whispered, "I think I wet my bed." I called the nurse in and we soon discovered what I thought had really taken place. Sure enough, her bag of water had broken. She was beginning to have some contractions now as well. Neither Jackie nor I would be going back to sleep any time soon. She did all right for the first few hours, but then it was very evident that this was not going to be a "natural" delivery. She began to beg for an epidural. "I'm never gonna get pregnant again!" she declared. "I just want this thing out!"

This was my little Johnnie's first day of school. With the way things were, I knew that I needed to stay with Jackie at the hospital. This meant that I was going to miss that moment of walking Johnnie to kindergarten and taking the first picture of him in his new uniform. I asked my friend Pilar to help me out with the "big event." She did a great job, and once I knew he was taken care of I could go ahead and concentrate on Jackie.

Jackie finally got the epidural that she'd been begging for and was able to sleep for a few minutes between contractions. She had gotten very tired. I wiped her brow and then fed her ice chips when she needed them. This was really a special day. It was 9-9-99, and soon Jackie would be slim and trim again while Clarissa would be holding her little princess in her arms.

Clarissa had a big box of Kleenex in her arms, as well as a video camera. Larry couldn't arrive until later that day as he had flown out to a job site early that morning. He actually flew in about thirty minutes before his new little princess would arrive.

At 4:18 in the afternoon, Denise Sara Winslow, rescue baby #169, was born. Clarissa cried and Larry praised Jackie. Denise weighed in at over 8½ pounds and was completely developed. Auntie Sara and Clarissa would take turns holding this precious little one. Baby Denise had the same little turned up nose as Jackie had.

I stayed in the room with Jackie as they finished cleaning her up. Baby Denise and her family went up to the nursery. I followed behind the gurney as the attendants moved Jackie to a different floor. There is no way that the baby should have to stay in with Jackie and there was no reason that she should have to remain on the floor and listen to everyone else's babies cry. I knew she needed a good night's rest and moving her would help her achieve that.

Once we got her settled in, Sara arrived with a beautiful bouquet of flowers. Jackie loved them and would look at them every once in a while as she drifted in and out of sleep. I stayed that night with Jackie. She had a pretty good evening. She still had one more thing she was craving that would be delivered after she got home from the hospital. She changed her mind the morning we were to leave. She decided that she wanted to see the daughter she had given birth to after all. Clarissa tried to be brave about it, but I knew she was dying inside. I explained that it would be a simple goodbye, so Clarissa didn't need to worry. No matter how much you say that to someone, it just isn't possible to get them convinced that this fear isn't necessary.

While Larry held onto Clarissa in the room they had occupied all night long with Baby Denise by their side, I pushed the wheel-chair containing Jackie. She was very quiet as the social worker guided us to a private room. There, in the center of the room was a little bassinette. Jackie stood to look at the baby. I asked Jackie if she wanted to sit down. "Sure," she said. I then went over and picked up the baby. I wasn't sure if she wanted to hold the baby or just look at her. I carried little Denise over to Jackie and sat down. "Would you like to hold her?" I asked. "Sure," she said. She immediately started to get a tear in her eye, "I don't know why I'm crying." I told her that it was okay; she probably had more feelings for this little girl than she thought she had. She told me that the reason she cried when she saw the baby after birth was because she saw the baby's feet and they reminded her of her boyfriend who was not the father of the baby.

Jackie only held the baby for about two minutes. Then she said, "Here, take her, I'm done." All the tears were now gone. I placed the baby back into the bassinet and helped Jackie get up. We walked back to her room and packed up the rest of her things. Legally, she had to leave the hospital before the baby and her new family could go home. Before we left, Auntie Sara arrived with a beautiful gift from Clarissa and Larry. It was a heart shaped pendant that held different types of stones such as sapphires, diamonds and topaz. It was so beautiful. It also had earrings to match. "Just a little something to say thank you for the precious gift," Sara stated. I was touched that they gave such a gift to such a precious woman. She deserved to be honored for making such a wonderful decision.

We drove on home that afternoon and Jackie waited for the one last thing she had been wishing for…a piece of mud pie from the Claim Jumper Restaurant. Not only did Sara arrive with a piece, but with the whole pie. If you have ever been to a Claim Jumper you know that one piece will fill a shoebox. Now, this girl had some serious work ahead of her.

✧✧ UPDATE ✧✧

Jackie was able to get her driver's license while in the Project Cuddle program. A car had been donated to the charity. We fixed it up and then she put in hours towards the purchase of the vehicle.

She moved back to the area she had grown up in, but not with her adoptive family. She called a few months ago and announced that she had fallen in love. Just recently we all helped in providing her with a wedding. The night before the big event we went to, of course, "Claim Jumper." After a huge meal, I asked if we were ready to go. "Not until I get my Mud Pie!" she proudly announced. I'll always remember Jackie whenever I see a Mud Pie.

Baby Denise is doing wonderfully. "Uncle Gino," also known as Gene Campbell, helped the Winslows put on an awesome luau to celebrate Denise's arrival to the family. At the end of the evening with tears in both Clarissa's and my eyes, baby Denise was presented to the guests. She and her new family attended the wedding of Jackie and her husband. For something borrowed, Jackie borrowed Clarissa's diamond earrings. Denise has already been traveling and in fact has gone to Europe just shortly after her first birthday. Mama Clarissa's side of the family lives there and the Aunt that Denise was named after was able to meet her for the very first time. Clarissa is thrilled to finally have her little Princess.

Jackie met with her family shortly after giving Denise up for adoption. They respect the decision she made and realize that she is very capable of caring for herself. Jackie has allowed her parents to see the son she just gave birth to. Things seem to be going well for Jackie and her new little family.

This Baby
Makes Seven

August 24, 2000

When we got the call about Isabella, we were a bit surprised. It wasn't the first time we had worked with an older woman, but it was the first time we worked with one who had so many children. Normally we find that fifty percent of our women/girls have at least one other child. The other forty-nine percent are pregnant with their first child. Isabella was now 40 years old and pregnant with her seventh child.

We actually got this particular call from an adoption agency. They had gotten a call from Isabella and couldn't get her convinced to meet with anyone or go to see a doctor. An attorney they often worked with called and asked if Project Cuddle could help. Of course we immediately said yes. Because she had no prenatal care at this point, she thought she was due in September. I was talking to my friend Pilar about meeting with her since she was the only one among us who spoke Spanish. My thirteen-year-old daughter Beth overheard this and told me she was willing to translate. Even though she was Hispanic, she didn't speak a word of Spanish. I asked her how she planned on doing this since she didn't speak the language. Everyone in the room had their ears perked up waiting to hear her answer. She confidently replied, "Well, I can do sign-language and spell the words." We all burst into laughter. She had had no idea this wouldn't work, or why we were laughing. We had to translate to her in English the explanation of why this wasn't possible. Then I thanked her for the offer. Pilar made a phone call to Isabella and asked to set up a meeting. It wasn't easy convincing Isabella that we could help her. She didn't want anyone to meet her at her house, in fact she wouldn't tell us where she lived. That following Saturday we asked her to meet us at a local drive-thru restaurant. She told us that she couldn't meet until she finished work, but that she would meet us at the location we had suggested as soon as she had finished. She would also be bringing her two-year-old son with her as well.

August 26, 2000

Pilar and I waited for 45 minutes in front of the restaurant. We were beginning to think that she wasn't going to show. We decided to give her another half hour just in case she was running late with her work or perhaps she had missed the bus. We saw a couple of pregnant women walk by and I am sure they looked at us in a rather strange way since we were definitely checking them out. Finally, we saw a woman that we were certain had to be Isabella. She was dressed in an old T-shirt and jeans. A little boy about two was holding her hand as she crossed the street. I remained in the "Cuddle Van" while Pilar went out to try and greet her. Sure enough, it was Isabella. She smiled at Pilar and they both headed toward the van.

Pilar introduced me as they climbed into the van. We asked Isabella what kind of food she was craving. She chose Mexican food. This was great! I took her to the best Mexican restaurant I know, "Mi Casa" in Costa Mesa. She ate chips as her son, Miguel, crawled under the table. She ordered cheese enchiladas but was only able to eat half of one. Miguel came up for a bit of food. He took a couple of chips and bounced up and down between Pilar and Isabella. About the third chip, Miguel choked. Isabella patted his back, but the chip didn't dislodge. Pilar grabbed Miguel and did the Heimlich maneuver. Fortunately, the chip did dislodge and Miguel was fine, but we kept the chips out of his reach.

Pilar and I asked Isabella some questions to find out what her situation was. She was now forty years old and pregnant with her seventh child. She was tired and getting too old to try and raise another baby. She didn't have any help with raising her children. She had never married. She didn't want anyone to know about this pregnancy and her teen children were due back from Mexico in twelve days. Isabella was a very proud woman. She still worked full-time cleaning houses. She was an illegal alien, so she couldn't get a better job. All her clients loved her and relied heavily on her services. She wasn't asking for anyone to give her a handout. She wanted to be proud of what she did and be able to say that she did it herself.

By the time we finished meeting with Isabella that day, we realized that she was really serious about keeping this situation a secret and not keeping this baby. We weren't even allowed to drop her off by her apartment, so we stopped about half a block away and let her and her son off. She had sent her two older children to Mexico for a visit with the grandparents and was anxious to have this baby delivered before her children returned. We made an appointment for her to see the doctor for the very first time that following Monday. She might only get to a doctor a few times before she delivered, but we needed to make sure that she and the baby were doing all right.

August 29, 2000

The newest staff member in our office, Jill, took Isabella for her first prenatal appointment. Jill didn't speak Spanish, but was willing to meet Isabella at the assigned corner and then smile at her and nod while taking her to her appointment and then back home. Sometimes all it takes is a friendly face or smile to help someone through a situation. This was one of those times.

The agency that had referred Isabella to us had run out of options in regards to families; she wasn't happy with any of them. She wanted a family that was nearby, that she could meet prior to the birth, and the agency only had families in Northern California. The agency had no other options and so they contacted the attorney who had told them about us. He was more than willing to help Isabella out by offering families. With this settled, we set up a meeting the following Friday and had Isabella meet with both the attorney and Pilar. They went over some more family profiles to hopefully find someone who met her specifications.

129

September 1, 2000

The Friday meeting took place just as planned. We met her at a local coffee shop. Isabella looked over the photos while Pilar read the letters from three different families. They were so different from each other. One had no children but they had two dogs. Isabella didn't like dogs and ruled them out right away because of this. The second family was a couple that had no children and had been through three miscarriages. The third couple had already adopted one child. Isabella listened quietly as Pilar read each one and showed no facial expressions during any of the letters. I waited along with the attorney as she picked up the photo of the second couple that Pilar and the attorney presented. She told Pilar that this was the one she wanted. She didn't need to look any further. In fact, she didn't even want to meet them before making this decision. She was determined that this was the final decision. The attorney wasn't comfortable with this. He wanted to allow both sides to meet before making a final commitment. So, we scheduled a meeting for Saturday morning at my home with the Moores.

We met at 10:00 a.m. in my home and all my children were running around just like they did every Saturday. Pilar had her two children there as well, and then of course Miguel joined right in with all the activities. Tyler was all dressed up as Davy Crockett that day. Miguel was fascinated by the raccoon hat and grabbed it off of our little "costume-boy's" head and took off in the backyard. Emily quickly ran out while laughing. She was still the nurturer and would make sure that they were all right. This made a grand total of eight children running around while the attorney calmly explained everything and went over some papers. This was one time that it was helpful working with an attorney who had twins. He didn't want the Moores to know that they had been chosen, only that they were being seriously considered. He felt that until he actually had them meet face to face, it wasn't a "done deal."

Isabella was very shy when she met the Moores. She wouldn't look up at them when they were introduced. She was very desperate to be accepted by them. She was afraid that they might change their minds and not take the baby. She really loved the adoptive couple from what she read in the letter and it turned out that this meeting would be a very memorable one that would reinforce her decision to go forward with this family. By the time they were done, she had chosen a wonderful family that lived only an hour a way and had waited anxiously for many years to adopt a baby. With Pilar translating, Isabella got all her questions answered and by the time the couple got ready to leave, Isabella asked Pilar to offer for them to adopt her baby who was about to be born. They were overjoyed and we all breathed a sigh of relief.

September 3, 2000

There were still many papers to be filled out and forms to be completed. Isabella would need to see an Adoption Service Provider immediately and the attorney was able to arrange for one who spoke Spanish. Things were looking up. The only real problem was the fact that Isabella hoped for this delivery before her son and daughter returned home from Mexico. We didn't have a true due date so we tried to help Isabella understand that we couldn't expect the doctor to induce her. We would have to wait until nature took its course.

September 5, 2000

It was only a day before Isabella's children were supposed to return to the states and Isabella didn't want them to find out about her little secret. Jill had planned to take Isabella for her California State Identification Card so she could get medical coverage. She was then scheduled to go to her second doctor's appointment. When Jill picked Isabella up, she looked very uncomfortable. Jill called on the cell phone and told me that she thought that Isabella might be in labor, but she wasn't sure. I told her to bring Isabella by the office and we would try and speak with her. I knew that Pilar would be available by phone.

Within fifteen minutes of receiving Jill's call, we saw Isabella enter the office. The poor thing had to climb the stairs in order to get to the office, and the look on her face told me she wasn't feeling well at all. She waddled on over to the sofa and slowly sat down. Her son on the other hand had enough energy for both of them and in true toddler form began to run around from place to place. He found stickers and stamps, paper and pen and tried putting them all to good use as quickly as he picked them up. Whatever was down at his level he grabbed it. It was funny watching Jill run behind him trying to gently take things from him before he hurt himself or the office. I asked Isabella how she was feeling. She told me she was all right. In my own broken Spanish, I told her that she needed to tell me the truth. She then proceeded to tell me that she had been up all night. She was tired and having pains every five to six minutes. I was surprised that they were so close together. I knew that since this was her seventh child, this baby could come very quickly and we needed to get her to the hospital immediately. Pilar wasn't available to take her into the hospital, so I looked over towards Angel and asked if she would like to be the one to coach in this delivery. Angel jumped at the chance. She then realized that she didn't speak any Spanish and was worried about that. I told her not to worry, that pushing is a universal language and she would do just fine.

We got Isabella back into the Cuddle Van and Angel drove towards Garden Grove Hospital. Jill took little Miguel over to where Pilar was working. She could watch Miguel for the next couple of days while Isabella had her baby and rested up.

I had worked with Angel before on coaching and in fact, she was mainly in charge of the delivery of our 200th baby. She had done so well that I felt confident in letting her do this one solo. She was a bit nervous, but excited as well. She called and checked in from time to time over the next few hours to let us know what was going on.

At first, Isabella didn't want anyone to touch her. Angel said, "At first, I offered my hand while she was sitting in the bed having a contraction. She didn't take me up on the offer. About a couple of hours later it was funny because she just reached out and picked up my hand and then put it into hers."

The Moores arrived just as she dilated to eight. It wasn't going to be much longer. She had gotten an epidural so she was relaxed enough and able to acknowledge them when they arrived. They stayed during the delivery, as did Angel. They shared in the baby's first breath, and first cry. It drew them all closer together. Isabella took a peek at the baby and then gave her a kiss on the forehead. She then held the baby out to the Moores. She spoke in Spanish and requesting that they take the baby away. The Moores and their new son, rescue baby #268, left the room. The hospital arranged for the family to have a room of their own. They would be able to get to know each other and have some privacy until the baby was ready to go home.

September 6, 2000

The following morning Isabella was released from the hospital. Pilar and I brought little Miguel along with us. Isabella had been transferred to a surgical floor so that she wouldn't have to hear the babies in the nursery crying. It was so great to see Isabella's eyes as they lit up when she saw her son. This was her baby. I took both Isabella and her son to my home and Pilar watched her while I went to get groceries. Miguel brought in a little cardboard box that he cherished very much. Jonathon had taught him the art of making money. David would offer each of our children a penny for each snail that they collected from the garden. So, Jonathon shared his little business venture with Miguel. Boy, was Isabella surprised when she looked in the box at his priceless treasure, a box of snails.

We transferred the groceries into Pilar's little red car and then placed Miguel in his car seat. She thanked me for the help and gave me a big hug. Miguel would go home now with his mother and soon be reunited with his siblings. He was too young to know what happened. It would be Isabella's secret alone.

✧✧ UPDATE ✧✧

Isabella is back at work now and her children are living with her in the room she rents. She is very happy with her decision and wouldn't change it for anything. We got to see the Moore's son recently when Mom and son came into the office. Each of the staff members got a real kick out of seeing the positive results to a case that we all worked so hard on.

Stuck With Hepatitis

July 2, 1999

The crisis line had been fairly quiet this week, but that phone can change everything in the blink of an eye. Our little "Costume-Boy" Tyler was deep in the throes of creativity this particular morning. He had gone into the restroom to take a shower just as any other normal eight-year-old. He seemed to be taking an unusually long time getting ready for the day, but I was pretty wrapped up with a crisis case in the living room so I didn't concentrate on Tyler.

I began taking down information on this frightened young woman. Her name was Jane Martin. She was 33 years old and a recovering drug addict. She had already given birth to three children. They were 10, 5 and 3 years old. She had been clean for almost a week now and knew that she needed to be seen by a doctor. By her estimation, she was probably due in about a month. By mine, I figured she was probably due any time. For some reason, many of the women in denial are actually about a month further along than they think.

Jane had not anticipated what she should do this time around. To complicate matters, the father of the baby wasn't her boyfriend. Her boyfriend was currently in prison serving time for dealing drugs. He had been incarcerated for a year and a half, so there was no way he could be the father. He had a violent temper and would probably go ballistic if he discovered what Jane had done.

Jane had gotten pregnant from a one-night stand. She was sure

135

she could not get pregnant because she was using drugs. The main rumor that seemed to spread among users was that using drugs was a form of birth control. Not true at all. In fact, during the thirteen years my husband Dave and I fostered babies, we fostered over 30 babies that were from drug-abusing mothers. Most of these women had at least four other children. All those babies showed me that this was a fallacy.

Jane's boyfriend was due to get out of jail in the next three months. He had a violent temper and the last thing she wanted was for him to abuse her or the baby when he got out of prison. She was so afraid of getting any prenatal care because she thought that they would take her other children away if she tested positive. What she didn't realize was that they would probably test both she and the baby, but that the baby would be the only one removed from her care if there were no signs of abuse or neglect with the other three.

I tried to explain to Jane that there were certain things that put up red flags for the hospital staff. The first red flag would be that she had no prenatal care. The second would be her jitteriness, and the third would be the track marks on her arms. If all three factors were present, they would definitely be doing some drug testing on both Jane and the baby.

I finished this conversation with Jane having accomplished something very important. She promised to allow us to take her to the doctor for her first prenatal appointment tomorrow. The doctor was so kind to allow us to come in on a Saturday. He knew how fragile Jane must be and he didn't want to risk her running.

July 3, 1999

I picked Jane up for her appointment at around 9:30 a.m. As she got into the front seat of the van, she noticed Tyler in the back seat. She did a double take and then smiled as she buckled her seat belt. Tyler was in true "Tyler form." He knew that the Fourth of July was the following day, so he decided that he should dress for the occasion. He had taken a plain red T-shirt and taped stripes of white tape around it. That part of his shirt looked just like an American flag's stripes. Then he took his blue acrylic paint and had painted the right sleeve completely blue. When it dried, he painted little white spots on the sleeve. These were his stars. Now the hat he was wearing was just like Abraham Lincoln's top hat, but it had red, white and blue on it.

"Happy Fourth of July!" Tyler declared to Jane. She wished him the same right back. We got to the doctor's office and spent some time there. He measured her belly and took the information she had given him to calculate her due date. As the doctor prepared to take blood, Jane said, "Oh, you might want gloves, I've got Hepatitis C." The doctor pulled rubber gloves from the box on the counter. He asked her how she had contracted the disease. Jane explained that she had been heavily into drugs for over fifteen years. She began using when she was eighteen. When she delivered her first child, that child tested positive for drugs. She lost custody of her child for almost two years. She was able to get her baby back, but found that she was always exhausted. She couldn't figure out what the problem was. She was afraid that she might have contracted HIV. The results came back from her tests and she was free of AIDS, but did test positive for Hepatitis C.

Her second child contracted Hepatitis C because she had no pre-natal care and delivered in an ambulance on the way to the hospital. He has suffered greatly ever since. She knew she could not possibly care for that child on her own, so she asked the baby's father to take custody. He has since married and this child has a great home with stability.

Jane's youngest child, Amy, was spared the dreaded disease. She was actually drug-free during that pregnancy and she went through all the prenatal visits from the second month of pregnancy on. She still has custody of Amy and her oldest child, Caleb.

The doctor told Jane that according to everything she had told him, she was due any time. We were instructed to take her over and pre-register her for the hospital. I had talked to Jane about what she was thinking of doing. She shared her plan with me on the way to the hospital. She knew that she was probably going to test positive for drugs. She knew that she would lose custody of the baby immediately if that happened and she didn't want the baby to spend years in foster care. She knew that she would have a hard time saying goodbye to it, but at least she would have some control over the situation. Not only that, but she would probably be saving herself and her children from being abused when Jane's boyfriend discovered she had been unfaithful. Yes, she was giving this baby up for adoption.

Tyler joined us at the registration booth. He wasn't sure why everyone was looking at him, but he smiled at everyone and wished them all a happy Fourth of July. Jane was getting such a kick out of Tyler. He talked about a mile a minute and was full of expression. He told her about the way our family celebrated the holiday and all the fireworks that his brother and father helped set off and how he hoped his dad would think he was big enough this year to help set them off.

We got the paperwork filled out and headed back towards home. She wasn't willing to let anyone know about her condition, so she asked that we drop her off at the neighborhood grocery store. I took her inside the store and purchased some food for her and the children. She was craving turkey, dressing and gravy. Needless to say, there wasn't any way I could defrost and cook a turkey in the next few hours, so I offered to buy some TV dinners. She thought that was a great idea and picked out two for her and one for each of her two children that lived with her. Tyler grabbed a bag of Oreos that he insisted we buy for their dessert.

I gave her a goodbye hug and then Tyler and I drove home. I promised to have the three families she had picked out of our books call her that evening. She knew her time was short and there was no time to waste. This would soon be all behind her. The families she was considering for adopting her baby were all very similar. They each had one other child and were from Catholic back-grounds. Because we didn't have much time on our hands, there wasn't time for her to pick families from other states. These fami-lies would have needed to have an Interstate Compact done and

138

time would not allow that. An Interstate Compact is an agreement between the sending state (where the mother is sending the baby from) and the receiving state (the state where the adoptive family is bringing the baby). This is another good reason to plan ahead when giving a baby up. It can open up your options to many more families.

I got a call on the crisis line at around 7:30 p.m. from Jane. She sounded so happy. She told me that she talked with all three families and was totally in love with the last one she spoke with. They were planning on meeting with her first thing in the morning. She then went on to tell me that she didn't want to worry me, but she thought that she might be in the beginning stages of labor.

July 4, 1999

I received a call at 9:30 in the morning. It was Jane. She had met with Betsy and Richard Reagan. They had been married for over fifteen years. Betsy had severe endometriosis at a very young age and had a hysterectomy before she was twenty. She went into a deep depression after that. She assumed that she would never be able to find anyone who would want to marry her since she wouldn't be able to have children.

Betsy enveloped herself with her work. She would stay late into the evenings and arrive early each morning. She was a wonderful employee. One uneventful morning Betsy was working at her desk and a very handsome young man came in with a delivery. She took one look at Richard and melted. As Richard approached her desk, he too felt something very special. He nervously asked if she was Betsy Adams. When she told him that she was, he told her that the package was for her and that he would appreciate it if she would sign for it. She smiled up at him and then she signed her name on the clipboard.

Betsy wished she'd had the nerve to speak up when she had the chance that day, but didn't. For the next few weeks she anxiously looked every time the door opened, hoping that Richard would come through again. Then she realized something. She should just order something from the same company and just maybe he would be the one to deliver it. Sure enough, three days later Betsy's dream came true. Richard came in and immediately went to her desk. "Hello Betsy, how are you today?" he sweetly asked. She smiled a beautiful big smile at Richard and then said, "Well I am doing just great Richard. What have you been up to?" This conversation was the beginning of a beautiful love between two people. Richard learned early on about Betsy's inability to bear children and his comment to Betsy upon discovering this was, "That's okay, we'll just adopt."

I immediately called the Reagans to let them know that they were about to become parents. Then I had the sad task of calling the other two families and letting them know that this wasn't going to be the baby for them. (I hate this part most of all.) The Reagan family got in touch with their attorney and began the paperwork.

I heard from Jane at 3:30 p.m. She was now in active labor. I asked Jill if she would like to coach in this delivery. She was excited at the thought and jumped at the opportunity. She was halfway there and I realized she had not taken a camera along with her, so I told her to stop by the gift shop and there would be one waiting for her.

I was so happy for the Reagans and this baby. Here, there had been no prenatal care, no ultrasound or amniocentesis to show whether the baby would even be healthy or not. Knowing that there was a chance that this child could end up with Hepatitis C and that this family was willing to love it unconditionally was incredible to me.

Because they wanted to keep the baby as safe as possible from contracting the disease, the doctors went ahead and did an emergency C-section. Jane did very well through this procedure. She delivered a beautiful little baby girl who weighed in at 7 lbs. 4 oz. that would be rescue baby #266.

The Reagan Family is very happy. They are about to become parents for the second time. Their little daughter was named Sunshine and has been every bit of that for this family. She has tested negative for Hepatitis and is very healthy.

Jane never told her boyfriend about this pregnancy. He is now out of jail and both he and Jane are currently off drugs. Jill stays in touch with Jane and keeps tabs on both of Jane's other children.

Chapter Six

How About Some Action?

Introduction

You may think that we deal with simple everyday situations, but I have found that when we least expect it, things seem to take a quick turn. We have had some very wild adventures. I want to share some of these with you in "How About Some Action?"

You will find that my life has completely changed, and for the good because of at least one of these situations. You will also discover that crisis situations can happen at any time and any place. Our goal is to be ready at a moment's notice to deal with them no matter what.

Baby abandonment is a daily occurrence as documented by COLORS 35 MAMA photo.

Baby #200 with his big brother, Baby #10. They are both loved dearly by their adoptive parents.

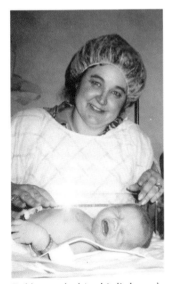

Debbe coached in this little one's delivery, baby #77, as she has so many over the years.

Baby #175 meeting her new family for the first time.

The headlines in the *Tulsa World* share the tragic tale of this baby's abduction and safe return.

Annie was raped and never expected this little Surprise package. Meet... Georgia.

Samantha, James & baby #71. At 14 she found herself pregnant. We helped her tell her mom who wanted to prosecute the 18-year-old boyfriend. We supported Samantha thru this and now she has graduated and are all happily living together.

Jonathon and his Daddy Dave at a Project Cuddle event.

Baby #115 survived the bowling alley incident and is happy and adopted.

CLIFF AGUILERA/For The Orange County Register

The headlines read, "Hunt for suspect empties bowling alley." Our family was there when this took place and fortunately it had a happy ending.

Debbe and her new granddaughter Abigail.

Baby #131 was only a couple of pounds at birth. She had no family to go to and the mother would be charged with abandonment if a friend had not decided to call Project Cuddle. Now she is in a great home.

The Basketball Babe's daughter, #311, and her new little brother.

Tyler with the secret baby, #199 that had been hidden for over seven months of pregnancy.

Baby #381, Mykayla, and her very proud Daddy Carl with Debbe and volunteer Tammy.

Baby Hope, #347, was smuggled out in a bag from her apartment where she was born. She was handed to Debbe and her family, naked and blue.

Sarah, #174, was hidden in a trailer from everyone for the first two weeks of her life.

Sarah's mother chose a great family and as you can tell, she is happy and safe in her new home.

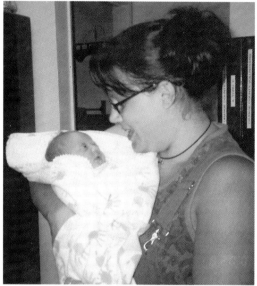

Co-worker Angel is an extremely vital part of Project Cuddle. Here she is with one of the little ones that she helped care for. I always say…she is truly an Angel!

Rescue Baby #169…the little princess.

Debbe and another "baby saver," Timothy Jaccard.

Rescued babies #22, #100, #122. All three are now in loving homes.

Emily and baby #12. He was born at home and smuggled out of the house in a laundry basket.

Tyler decided on a wardrobe as a vendor this particular day. He sold light bulbs and paper plates to the family.

The Magnusen Family (L to R) Tyler (11), Emily (14), Jonathon (7), Bejay (15), Beth (15), Dave holding Granddaughter Abigail, Debbe, Lani (24), Brian (25) and his wife Talea.

Babies #386, #381, and #402 posing for the camera.

Tyler in his costume of the day. He is a duck.

Bonding at Gunpoint

May 29, 1998

The crisis line rang and I picked it up, but this time there was someone at the other end of the line for just a moment, then they hung up. About fifteen minutes later I got another call, and when I asked the person on the other end of the line if they needed help, she very quietly said, "Yes." I found out that her aunt referred this young lady to us. In fact, even though the girl was from Texas, her aunt lived only a few miles from me. The caller was very scared. I knew that I was going to have to do a lot to reassure her that everything was okay.

Talea had been a little Korean baby adopted by an American family from Texas. She was only four months old when she came to the states, but was greeted with open arms by her father, mother and big brother. Talea's mother had longed for a little daughter to call her own. But because she was a polio victim who was now a paraplegic, with only partial mobility of her arms, she wasn't allowed to adopt through the country. This was such a big deal when she did finally get to adopt that the local paper made it a front-page story. Talea still has that newspaper article. It shows her mother in a wheel chair with little Talea on her lap. Her mother was very capable of raising Talea and did so until Talea was eighteen. Then, things changed. Talea noticed a small lump on the back of her mother's head. She commented to her mother, "Mom, you should probably get that checked out. Maybe it's cancer or something." She actually was joking. Within a week, she would find out the terrible truth. Talea's prediction was right on target—her mother had brain cancer.

Talea is very intelligent. She had graduated early, then became a nursing assistant. She then cared for her mother. She would change her dressings, decorate her hospital rooms when she had to go in, coordinate her visitation schedule and lie by her mother's side to comfort her. She had done this for over a year. Unfortunately, the cancer was too far advanced. Talea's mother knew that she didn't have much time left. She wanted to spend those last months with her precious daughter. She wanted to share some of those moments that she knew she was going to miss out on. They began to plan for Talea's wedding. They picked colors and flowers, styles of dresses and the type of ring Talea wanted. No, she didn't have the man of her dreams yet, just a boyfriend that she liked. But, she wanted her mother to be a big part of her choices even if she couldn't be there. They also planned her mother's funeral; what songs would be sung, what type of casket. Her mother even wrote a poem that was to be printed on little business cards and laminated for each guest. It told of how she wanted everyone to rejoice. She wanted everyone to remember that she was now in Heaven. She would be able to walk, feel no pain, and wait to see each of her family members one day.

Her mother died and Talea found herself very depressed. She had spent so much time focusing her energies on her mother that she had basically stopped everything that revolved around her. Now that her mother was gone, she leaned on her boyfriend. Talea was extremely vulnerable. Both her brother and her father were suffering as well. The only person she felt she could go to for comfort was the boy she had been dating off and on for the past year. At this time she found herself intimate with him. She was so devastated by the loss of her mother that she didn't even pay attention to the fact that she had missed her period for a few months. The holidays came and went, but it just wasn't the same without her mother. Talea just couldn't seem to get on her feet.

It wasn't until March that Talea was talking with her girlfriend and figured out that perhaps she was pregnant. She had been raised in a very strict Christian home. This wasn't going to be acceptable to anyone in the family. Not only that, but the baby was going to be half-black. She and her girlfriend bought a couple of home pregnancy tests. They were so scared to see the results that they left the room after leaving the test on the bathroom sink. They both went back into the bathroom and turned the light on. When they saw the results they both screamed. They just couldn't believe that they saw a positive test result. So they tried the second test, just hoping that this was all a mistake. The second test again told them that she was pregnant. There was no denying it now.

Talea's girlfriend was finally able to get her to an adoption agency. She gave the agency all kinds of information about herself. The very last thing mentioned was the fact that the baby would be half-black. As soon as this was divulged, the whole attitude of the woman changed. "I'm sorry, but this won't be easy. In fact, if we can't find a family, or if the baby is defective, it will be placed in an institution." This wasn't an option for Talea's baby. She was so disheartened. She didn't know what to do. She was being pressured by her girlfriend to tell her father and aunt. She was starting to show and wasn't going to be able to hide it any longer. She called her father and told him the bad news. He was shocked, but told her he would stand by her. She told him that she had no plans on keeping the baby. She went to another agency and heard the same thing all over again. There were no black families in Texas to take this baby and the Caucasian families wouldn't be interested considering that most of the area was white. The Asians wouldn't be interested either. It was time to call her aunt. Talea had no idea how she would take this whole thing, but without her mother around, she felt she had no options. Talea called her Aunt Lanore in southern California. She talked about all kinds of things, just trying to avoid the real subject. Eventually, she ran out of things to talk about. She went ahead and shared her deep dark secret. Her aunt was very kind and said that she had the phone number of a program that could help. She gave Talea the number and made her promise to give them a call.

The first time she called, she hung up. She knew she had to follow through because she promised her Aunt that she would. She waited a couple of hours and then called back. This time I answered the phone and she finally replied. I had to pull information from her. When I finally asked her name, she told me it was Talea.

She explained that it is pronounced like Ta-lay-a. I was in a great mood that day and began singing her name to the music from the "West Side Story" song entitled "Maria". I just added Talea's name in the place of Maria. She and I both began to laugh. I was happy that she liked it and I began to relax a bit.

Talea explained to me that she was pregnant and felt that no one wanted her baby. Not only did we have the race issue, but also she had a very specific list of things she wanted in a family. I knew that it wouldn't be the easiest of cases, but I knew that we would be able to help her. I told her that she didn't need to worry, we would help her get through this. She left the conversation relieved and hopeful. Sometimes there are girls that you feel exceptionally drawn to. This was the case with Talea. I promised her that I would do everything in my power to support her through this pregnancy and beyond.

It was clear that she couldn't stay in Texas. She was miserable in the heat and spent most of her time alone since her brother had joined the service and her father was working over 60 hours a week. She didn't want the father of the baby to come back and find out where she was. He had evidently been seeing someone else during the same time he was seeing her. She spoke with her father and her aunt and decided that she would come out to California. Because we didn't know exactly when she was due, we thought we had better get her out fairly soon. I spoke with her father on the phone and he agreed that at least out here she would be able to have support that he couldn't give her.

June 29, 1998

Talea was on her way to California. When I asked her how I would recognize her, she chuckled and said, "I have the smallest eyes in the world." I told her that Asians do typically have smaller eyes, but I still wouldn't be able to see the difference. She was serious when she said that hers were the smallest. She explained that sometimes people thought she was sleeping, or not looking at them because her eyes seemed to be closed. I got a brief description of what she was wearing. I told her we would meet next to the statue of John Wayne. It was only going to be a couple of days until we finally met. We had spent so much time on the phone together, that I felt as though I truly knew her. One of the girls who had been staying with us for the past month by the name of Anna was excited that she would have a friend in similar circumstances.

I called Talea three days before she was to come out. She wasn't home that day, but I left a message for her to call me when she got in; there were a few last minute details to go over. A couple of hours later, I received a call from "Miss T." "Hi Debbe, it's me," she proclaimed. I wasn't sure if it was her so I asked. When she told me it was, I explained that she sounded so different. She told me that she was on a cell phone in Missouri shopping for clothes. I couldn't figure out what she was doing all the way up there. She told me that they have good shopping there and that she didn't want anyone in Texas to see that she was pregnant. Now, that's what I call shopping!

The day finally came for her to arrive. She called me bright and early that morning to tell me she was on her way to the airport. She was so excited. Anna was just as excited. I knew that Anna was very anxious so I wanted to give her something to work on while waiting for her new friend to arrive. I brought out a roll of white paper and then wrote "Welcome Talea" on a sheet of it. Anna then colored it in. This was the sign that Anna could hold up for Talea to see. I took a few of the children to the airport to help in welcoming her. Anna was in the front seat with the sign on what was left of her lap. After all, she was due in the next month. There was no parking available when we got to the airport, so I dropped Anna off at the entrance to the baggage claim.

I must have circled the airport at least twenty times. Finally, two very pregnant girls emerged from the baggage claim area. They were dragging the biggest duffel bag that I had ever seen in my life. It was about five feet long and three feet high. These two were literally dragging it. I pulled up to the curb and my son Bejay got out and helped them put it into the back of the van.

We arrived home and Talea went into the living room to rest.

She laid down on the "Bette sofa" and put her feet up. About ten minutes after arriving, she made a call to her father and aunt to let them know that she had arrived safely. As she was finishing up the second phone call she got startled by little Tyler who was then seven years old. He walked over to her in a bright yellow rain slicker, goggles and adult-sized boots. "Hi, I'm Tyler. Who are you?" She tried to keep a straight face as she told the person on the other end of the line that she was just greeted by "costume-boy." She got off the phone and talked with him for a minute. Then Tyler went on to play.

Finding the right family for Talea's baby wasn't going to be easy. She reviewed over 70 families before finding the right one. She spoke with many families on the phone. She found a few of these families interesting and decided to meet them for dinner or lunch. Each one met and spent a few hours talking about their hopes for a child as well as Talea's hopes and dreams for her baby. No family seemed to be good enough for her. There wasn't much time left. She would soon need to find the right family or risk this baby going into foster care. I knew that Talea didn't want that, but I chose not to remind her of the time situation because I didn't want her making a decision on a family for the wrong reason.

June 30, 1998

I let our Board of Directors know about the problem we were having. I let friends and neighbors know as well. They in turn would tell their friends that we needed to find families that would be introduced to Talea and were interested in adopting an Asian, African-American baby. It worked within a couple of days. We got a call from one of our Board members, Mary Hibbard. Mary spoke very highly of a family that had been married for twenty years. They had helped in raising their niece and nephew, but never were able to have a child of their own. They didn't care if the baby was pink with polka dots; they just wanted to love a baby. We set up a meeting for that following Saturday. Perhaps this would be it.

August 1, 1998

Saturday morning came. I woke up with a horrible migraine. There was no way I wanted to go to lunch. I asked Talea if she would mind if I didn't go. She told me in no uncertain terms that she needed for me to go. If I wasn't going, she didn't want to go either. So I went, along with five of my children, Talea, Anna and the prospective family and their grown niece Janet that they had raised and her fiancé. That brought the total to eleven. I was very quiet as we walked into the local "Coco's" Restaurant. We must have looked like a stampede as we entered the lobby area. Talea and Anna went right up to the counter where they displayed beautiful pies and cakes. They just stared into the case as we waited for our table. I just stood there as we waited for them to set up a table for us. I saw my favorite waitress, Debbie Powell, behind the counter. Barely able to function, I picked up my head to say hello. It was weird. She didn't respond as she normally had. I commented to one of the kids how it was as though she didn't recognize me. I thank God I had a migraine. It may have saved my life. Normally if Debbie saw me she would say hello and would immediately ask me what I was currently involved in. She did not respond like that at all this time. If I had been feeling well, I would have gone up to the counter and asked, "Are you alright?" Instead, I just sat down. I commented to my daughter Emily that Debbie was acting so strange, but I did not pursue it. Talea and Anna were still drooling over the desserts. All of the sudden, Talea got bumped and in turn bumped into Anna. Then a man ran out from behind the counter and bolted through the front door. I was only half paying attention at this point, but I noticed that the waitress who had ignored me was calling 9-1-1. "We've just been robbed!" she shouted. I couldn't believe what I was hearing. If I had leaned forward as she stood behind that cash register, I would probably have been shot. He had been standing there with the gun at her as she emptied the money into a bag. Evidently this guy had been waiting for 2½ hours to try and find the right moment to rob this establishment. I guess when he saw our huge group come in he didn't think that he would be noticed.

We were all seated as the police sirens came closer toward us.

Talea kept right on track as she began to ask questions about this family. They seemed to have a lot of the answers she was looking for and it seemed as though this might be "the one." Stacey and her husband Chuck were sweet people. Stacey was a florist and Chuck owned a bagel and cappuccino drive-thru. They really loved each other and were thrilled at the thought of even being considered for this baby. I could tell that they had done a great job in raising Janet and knew that this was a great family for Talea to be considering. As we began to get the food we had ordered, we noticed that all the attention outside the restaurant was on the bowling alley across the street. Evidently the robber had gone inside the bowling alley in order to get away from the police. It didn't work. Through the main course and into the dessert, the police were crouched down on the ground behind their police units with their guns and rifles drawn. I think that meal brought Talea closer to this particular family. As we left the restaurant, the guns were still drawn, and I made the children stay next to me and I grabbed Jonathon back towards my side until we got into the car.

On the way home, I asked her what she thought about the family. She told me that this was the one. We began to think of a special way to tell them that they had been chosen. I remembered Stacey was a florist. Since I had been a florist, I knew how much I loved flowers and how I never seemed to get any. Perhaps we could get flowers delivered to her with a note from Talea congratulating her on the upcoming birth of her baby. Talea liked the idea, but hoped that we could get pictures of the moment. We talked to Stacey's niece and she helped us arrange everything. Janet asked her aunt to meet her at the church. She told her she needed to talk. Once there, Stacey's husband, Chuck arrived and together at the request of Janet they sat down on a bench. Janet then presented the flowers to Stacey. The photos would soon arrive to Talea and would reveal the utter shock and joy as Stacey had read the card. It just seemed impossible to Stacey that her dream of being a mother was about to come true.

August 14, 1998

For the next couple of weeks Talea and Anna would lie on the

152

sofa, watch soap operas and eat popsicles. They were like twins and did everything together. We would take them shopping, to church and to parties. Since we had two small boys in the house, each of the girls attached herself to one of the boys. Talea grew very close to Jonathon and Anna to Tyler. Each boy would cuddle with his "girlfriend." They would talk to the girl's tummies and rub them once in a while.

Neither one of these girls had ever made a turkey dinner. So, I decided that since we usually made a turkey at least once a month, we would go ahead and purchase two small ones and they would each prepare one. They were excited at the thought of doing this. Then, the reality of taking the necks and gizzards out got both of them a little freaked out. They both giggled and squealed as they emptied the turkeys' cavities. They proceeded to pick their turkeys up by the wings and made them dance to the music on the radio. They were quite a sight. That night we all dined on a good old-fashioned dinner. They had prepared the stuffing, mashed potatoes and finally I taught them how to do the gravy. It all tasted delicious. Now they would be able to duplicate this for their families someday.

Our freezer had never been opened and closed as much as it now was. Popsicles disappeared faster than speeding bullets. The girls began to settle in and realized that there was more to life than just television. They decided that they wanted to help me out with the phones and mailings. It was great. Anna had the best handwriting I'd ever seen and Talea was great on the telephones. I would take the initial calls, but then I would ask the callers if they would like to talk to one of the girls in the program. It seemed to help both girls involved in the conversation. The new girl would realize that she wasn't the only one going through this; that she wasn't alone. Then Talea or Anna would discover that because of what they had gone through they could give back and help others who weren't as far along.

July 22, 1998

Finally, at around noon, Anna started to have labor pains. She

153

was now two weeks overdue and very huge. We knew it was going to take some time for things to really get started, so we took the kids to the pool for one last swim. Anna sat and relaxed on a lounge chair. By five in the evening, her contractions were getting closer. I was now timing them and when she would have one, she would just hit me with the back of her hand. She didn't feel much like talking, so a hit would do. I must admit that it shocked me. I always thought of Anna as the passive one and yet, I was getting the wrath of her contractions. I wanted her to get to the hospital so that she could get something for the pain. I knew that they were now ten minutes apart, so this was a good time for the kids to get out of the pool and a good time for us to head up to the city of Orange. Unfortunately, she didn't want to go yet. Then I reminded her that her favorite nurse, Farrah was working this day, but only for one more hour. When I mentioned Farrah's name, she perked up and said, "Let's go!" So, we loaded up the kids, their towels and their wet bodies and headed towards home. Even though she was two weeks overdue, she hadn't packed a bag for the hospital. (It's amazing, but this is something I found happened quite often. The girls didn't want to think about it or acknowledge what was coming.) So we quickly put things in a duffel bag and headed out the front door. Talea would now help Dave take care of the children while Anna delivered. Then when it was Talea's turn, Anna would help with the kids.

Because Anna had chosen to give her baby up for adoption, I knew that she would need some extra emotional support. (I personally stayed with her before, during, and after she delivered and until she came home.) We called the adoptive family while in the car. They had waited so very long for a baby. We still didn't know if it was going to be a boy or a girl, but we knew that this had been a seven-year wait for Larry and Karlene Gentley. It just so happened that Larry was a respiratory therapist at the hospital where Anna was going to deliver. He and Karlene headed for the hospital where they would anxiously sit and wait to find out if they had a daughter or a son.

They tried to give Anna an epidural, but it didn't work. They had given her Pitocin to help get the contractions going. Unfortunately, the medication caused her more problems. She ended up with one constant contraction. I have never seen anyone suffer so much while in labor. The doctor just couldn't get the right injection site for the epidural. He struggled for an entire hour trying to get it in. It was awful! She was having contractions during this whole procedure and suffering horribly. The obstetrician finally came in to evaluate the situation. Anna wasn't progressing at all. He realized that she would need a C-section in order to get this baby out.

It wasn't long after that Anna went into the operating room and she was out of pain. She then delivered a beautiful, healthy baby girl. It was Project Cuddle's 100th baby as well. We were all so relieved. This was a big baby. She had full little cheeks and a great set of lungs. The Gentleys were ecstatic. This was the little girl that Karlene had always dreamed of.

July 23, 1998

That following morning, Dave brought Talea, Tyler and the other kids up to see Anna and the baby. They each took turns talking to Anna. Tyler sat next to her on her bed. After a good visit with her, they went downstairs to the nursery where they got their first peek at little Mariah. Talea took a few pictures and then they headed on home. It wouldn't be too much longer (we hoped) and Talea would be here.

Later that day, I went with Anna down to see her baby for the first time. I asked her if she wanted the Gentleys to leave the room before she got there. "No, it's their baby, they can stay." As we approached the room I could see that Larry was carefully holding his new daughter. I could tell that they were a bit uncomfortable and not sure what they should do. I said, "Hello Mom and Dad. Look who's here to see your baby." That loosened things up. They realized that she wasn't a threat and just wanted to see the baby. They placed the baby in the incubator and then came over to give Anna a hug. They gave her the love and respect she so deserved. We took a few photos of the moment and then sought out Farrah. She would be the one in the final photo taken of that memorable day.

155

July 26, 1998

Though Talea felt as big as a whale, the baby just wasn't mature enough to be delivered. The movie "The Titanic" was very popular then. Talea would say, "I'm not going to give birth to a baby; this is the Titanic." She felt so miserable. She fussed a lot more than Anna. I think part of it was just her personality and also the fact that she was much shorter, so there wasn't anywhere for the baby to go except out.

August 26, 1998

We all went to the baby shower that was taking place for Stacey's new baby-to-be. The theme was Noah's Ark and everything she received could be for a boy or a girl. Though most pregnant girls don't usually go to their adoptive family's baby shower, Talea wanted to. We had a good time and walked out of there knowing that this baby was going to have a lot of love from a lot of people.

September 21, 1998

Two months after Anna gave birth, Talea was still pregnant. The doctor told us that if she didn't deliver in the next three days, we would have to induce her. Two days later I had a very sick feeling. It was like a sixth sense. I knew in my gut that there was something wrong. I asked Talea if she was feeling the baby move. "A little, but not nearly as much as normal." I didn't want to alarm her, but I asked her how she would feel about going ahead and seeing the doctor today instead of tomorrow. She said that this would be fine. She would love to get "Shamu" out sooner rather than later.

September 23, 1998

We went on to the doctor's office. He checked her over and told us that we could either have this baby born today or tomorrow. It was now up to us. Talea looked at me and I again reiterated my concerns. "Okay, let's do it today," she announced. I felt immediate relief. We were soon guided by our favorite nurse, Farrah, into a labor room. In a couple of hours the doctor started to give her medication that would cause her to go into labor. Before the following morning Stacey and Chuck would be holding their new baby.

Stacey and Chuck arrived as Talea's contractions began to get stronger. I asked them if they had chosen a name. They told me Noah Michael if it was a boy and Kelsey if it was a girl. They hadn't chosen a middle name yet. We started coming up with middle names as Talea kept coming up with more contractions. "How about Maddison?" I asked. They said that they liked it.

At around 7:00 p.m. the doctor came in and told Talea that the baby's heart rate wasn't doing very well. Every time she had a contraction it would slow the baby's heart rate down. They stopped the Pitocin and told Talea that she would have to go in for a C-section. She realized that this was crucial for saving her baby. Talea asked to be awake so that I could be with her during the delivery. It was all set. By 8:00p.m. we were getting ready to wheel Talea into the operating room. She and Anna had become good friends with my oldest son Brian over the past few months. Before she went into the operating room she wanted to say goodbye to Brian. They waited as long as they could. The doctors were now waiting for her. As they pulled the gurney out of the labor room and into the hall, there came Brian. Talea was a bit delirious, but thrilled that he made it in time. (He had gone to Hoag Hospital in Newport Beach by mistake. The weirdest thing about that was that his newest cousin had just been born there that afternoon and he wasn't even aware of it yet. He finally called the hot line to find out which hospital we were in.)

We went on into the delivery room and I held her hand as she was prepared for surgery. She began to shake as she realized what was about to happen. I rubbed her brow and spoke to her as the doctors started the procedure. I was the first one to see Kelsey Maddison Veach, rescue baby #115, as she was born. She had a great set of lungs and was screaming all the way over to the pediatric nurse. "I don't want to hear it cry. Stop the crying," Talea begged. I looked at the anesthesiologist and asked him to please increase her medication so she wouldn't hear this. He told me that he would give her something so she would forget this moment. As they finished stitching her up, I went with the incubator containing baby Kelsey; we headed for the nursery and Kelsey's new family. I could see them all in the distance. "Would you like to see your new daughter?" I asked as the incubator was wheeled closer. Stacey broke down in tears and Chuck stood behind her and held onto her as their new daughter passed by. The nurse paused for just a moment so that they could take their first peek. They all watched as the pediatrician checked her out. The little one who was dubbed "the Titanic" weighed in at only 6lbs., 4 oz. Boy, was Talea going to be mad when she found out how tiny Kelsey was!

September 24, 1998—midnight

I went back up to the ICU and stayed with Talea until the next morning. We then transferred to a floor that was completely away from the nursery. (I knew that Talea wanted to go down and see the baby, but would wait until she asked to go.)

Talea made a very quick recovery and wanted to walk down to see the baby within 16 hours of having her. She asked that only she and I be in the room at that point. Just as we got ready to leave the room, the social worker for the hospital showed up and wanted to speak with Talea alone. I told them I would go on downstairs and ask the Veachs to step out of the room so she could have some privacy. Stacey and Chuck were sitting there doting on their new daughter when I showed up. I could tell that Stacey didn't want to leave the baby's side, even for a moment. I heard Talea down around the end of the hall. This meant that I had no way of getting the Veachs out of the section we were in without being seen by Talea. I had to think quickly. I went across the hall and checked to see if there was a vacant room. Almost...I found one full, and I do mean full of chairs, beds, wheelchairs, etc. I quickly told Stacey and Chuck to hide in there. Once I closed the door to the room with Talea inside, they could step out and go out of the area and into the lobby. It was like something seen in a movie.

Talea came in and saw Kelsey for the first time. She had a tear

158

in her eye, but did very well. I asked if she would like to see her toes and hands. She said, "Sure." I set the baby down on the bed and slowly unwrapped her. "She has such long toes," Talea commented. Then we continued to inspect the small baby for a few more minutes. She was so happy the baby had bigger eyes than she. Tyler soon entered the room along with Anna, Jonathon and Dave. Each got a turn holding baby Kelsey.

Talea told me when she was ready to leave this room and go on back upstairs. She again insisted upon walking. She had so much determination. She knew what she wanted to do and was going to do it. I was proud of her for that. Within a few days you could hardly tell that she had gone through a C-section. She endured the pain so well.

Talea stayed with us in our home for four months after the delivery. She went on to work for Project Cuddle for the next nine months. During that time she was able to help many girls and women who were frightened and in need of help.

✧✧ UPDATE ✧✧

I am now a mother-in-law. You might ask what that has to do with this story. Remember, I spoke of my son Brian and how he became Talea's good friend. Well, this friendship blossomed and after a year-and-a-half of dating, they became engaged. A snowy, winter wedding in Chicago of 2000 brought Talea permanently into the Magnusen Family as she married my son Brian. They became parents to a beautiful baby girl almost a year later. I have a new title...Granny. Thank you Brian and Talea!

My Little Internet Girl

Shortly after appearing on the Oprah Winfrey Show, we received quite a few cases of frightened, pregnant girls from our website on the Internet. I have found that it has been a very new and challenging way to rescue babies. The main difference with girls on the Internet is that somehow you have to help the girl understand that you truly do care, and yet without any verbal contact it is difficult to get the emotion across to each girl.

We have now rescued three babies and their mothers via the Internet, and still, I get headaches every time I have to work on another. Don't get me wrong—I am thrilled that girls who are too frightened to call will at least take the proper steps to contact me in this manner. It's just that when one contacts us, I can't hear her voice or see her face in order to know that I am actually getting through to her. I hope that with time, I will learn, as I did with the first phone cases, what works and what to avoid when trying to work with Internet girls.

April 28, 2000

I received an e-mail from one particular young lady that tore at my heart. She signed her letter as "Scared and Alone." She told me how she was fifteen years old and no one knew her horrible secret. She was about six months pregnant with no prenatal care. She was a good girl by normal standards. She got As and Bs in school and worked after school at a corner market. She made one mistake. She met a young man by the name of Eddie. He worked at the corner market as well. He was the son of a preacher. He didn't hate God and church, but he did find ways to rebel against some

161

of the Ten Commandments. He was picked on at school because his dad was this little town's preacher. Somehow Eddie wanted to prove to the kids that he was cool. He had been going out with "Scared and Alone" for almost six months. They would go to school dances separately and then meet up once they got there. That way Eddie wouldn't get in trouble for dating when he was considered too young, and "Scared and Alone" would do the same for the exact same reasons. They got way too close, and it was probably because they were each rebelling in their own way. "Scared and Alone" would soon learn the hard way that her parents had a reason for setting down rules and curfews.

For over two and a half months I tried to convince this poor frightened girl to call the toll-free number. There was no way she was willing to do this. I finally got her to contact one of our volunteers in her area over the Internet. I also gave her the e-mail address of adoption attorney Steven Lazarus. He was willing to donate his time to write her on the Internet if she would just write him. Natalie, a new volunteer, struck up a friendship and soon I knew that Natalie would be one of the ones to help "Scared and Alone" through the rest of her pregnancy. She wrote to Steven within a couple of days. He sent a Fed Ex of family bios to Natalie of those willing to work with "Scared and Alone" if she was interested. We knew that this was a big step. She was now communicating with three people on the Internet. No, this wasn't the best way, nor was it an easy way to work with her, but it was all we had.

By the time that this young lady was 7½ months pregnant, she finally gave us her first name. It was a day that the whole office staff celebrated. Her first name was Katie. She still hadn't gotten to a doctor, but we knew now that she had no intention of keeping this baby. Evidently, she lived with her mother and her stepfather. Her mother was a fragile woman and very submissive to her new husband. Katie knew that if her stepfather ever found out that she was pregnant, it would be the perfect excuse for her to be kicked out. She couldn't survive on her own, so she needed to get rid of this baby. Now that she had found us, she felt a weight lifted off her shoulders. Unfortunately, I wasn't feeling quite as relaxed as she. The pressure was on us as we still hadn't had any verbal contact with her and she still had no prenatal care. I really wanted a better gauge on things, and then I would relax...a little.

June 12, 2000

I finally received the call I had been hoping for. "Hi Debbe, this is Natalie," the voice said on the other end of the line. "Hi Natalie, how are you doing?" I asked her. I knew that she and Katie had a tentative meeting scheduled for this particular day, but couldn't tell by her voice whether or not she was calling to say that Katie had not shown or that she had shown. Well, Katie had shown and was standing next to her, waiting to speak with me. "Hi honey," I said as I began to cry. "You have no idea how many people have been worried about you and praying for you. You are truly loved and cared about." Natalie later told me that as I was speaking with Katie she got tears in her eyes. She and I spoke for the next five minutes. I told her that I was coming out the following week to film the "Ricki Lake Show" and wanted to meet with her. She said this would be fine. I encouraged her to look over the letters and photos that Steven had sent her. If there weren't any there that she wanted to talk to, that would be okay, but we were running out of time. I hoped that she would at least begin to focus on the fact that she was about to have a baby and she needed to make some decisions on what she wanted to do.

June 19, 2000

One week after that phone call was placed, I was taking the New Jersey Transit system from New York to New Jersey. There I would wait at the train station as instructed in order to get a glimpse of our little Katie. I had Lani and Tyler with me on this trip and they went on sightseeing as I waited. I had no real idea what this girl would look like, so I was hoping that she would recognize me. I had spoken with her the night before, and asked her, "Didn't you see me on Oprah?" She told me that she had. "Okay then, I will wear the same pink outfit that I wore on that show."

This particular train station was so small that it wasn't even open. Fortunately the rain cloud that loomed overhead just loomed and didn't decide to let go as I sat there. Just at 4:00 p.m. a young girl with a sweatshirt and jeans walked towards me. I wasn't sure if this could be her or not. I looked at her and she looked back at me. I thought that I would give one more look and if she again returned that look I would ask, "Katie?" She nodded sheepishly. I stood up as I said, "Hi honey." And we then embraced. She was really here and she looked really good.

I handed her the papers that I had been given for her to fill out. There were authorizations for medical records and history questions about the father of the baby and herself. This took her the better part of an hour to fill out. We sat on the bench and talked as she filled out the records. She was a sweet-looking girl with long, sandy blond hair and big blue eyes. She seemed rather quiet. When she came to the part of the questionnaire that asked her personality, I noticed that she put down the word, "outgoing." I was truly surprised at this so I said, "Wait a minute. You mean to tell me that you are outgoing but you couldn't dial our number?" I then smiled at her and she giggled. "Well, I am outgoing," she proclaimed. "Well then don't be afraid silly-willy to call our toll free number," I said with a smile. "I won't be afraid now," Katie told me. I was glad to hear that. We chatted until the train arrived to take us back to New York. Lani and Tyler were just coming back from their excursion and small drops of rain were just beginning to fall. It was all so perfect. I would take the information that I had now obtained and fax it to the attorney. Once this was done, I would rely on Natalie to be my eyes and ears. She would stay in touch with Katie until after she delivered. I had quizzed Katie on what she would do when she went into labor. I also gave her some signs to look for that she might otherwise ignore. I didn't want this precious little girl or her baby to end up as statistics.

June 21, 2000

Two days after I met with Katie she met the family she had chosen to adopt her baby. They came in from another state and from what I heard, everything went quite well. I was relieved to know that both parties involved were excited about this baby being placed into the Wilson's home. Now it was a matter of only a few more days of waiting. I longed to have that call come through to me. Natalie had all my numbers, so now we would play the waiting game.

✧✧ UPDATE ✧✧

One week after meeting with Katie, we got the call we had been waiting for. She had gone into labor last evening and didn't tell anyone. The stepfather whom Katie had been so fearful would kick her out, helped her deliver the baby. Her stepfather called Natalie to let her know that they had just called 9-1-1 and that they would help Katie. She was taken by ambulance in the wee hours of the morning to the nearest hospital.

The attorneys for both parties began the paperwork and within twenty-four hours of this little girl's birth, she would be in a home filled with lots of love. I spoke with Katie on the phone this evening. She sounded so relieved. I asked her if things were all right with her stepfather. She told me that they were. He would not kick Katie out of the house. This had brought her and her mother closer together as well.

This was truly a joint effort. It took Oprah airing information about our program, the knowledge of attorney Steven Lazarus, and the diligent work and sensitivity of the Project Cuddle staff and the local volunteer. The wacky world of the Internet had now helped in rescuing a baby. Baby Madeline, rescue baby #276, is now safe and Katie has her whole life to look forward to.

Trick or Treat?

Halloween 1999

It was just beginning to get dark outside and Jonnie was anxiously waiting for me to put the finishing stitches on his costume. He was borrowing Tyler's Tigger costume from the year before and hated the fact that he could not be a Ninja like he wanted. Tyler wasn't very happy with the fact that his little brother was borrowing his Tigger clothes. We still see Tyler wear them to bed on a cold winter night, and after all...he is the family Tigger.

The crisis line began to ring as I zipped up the back of Jonnie's suit. It was a call from a woman who needed help right away. She had been in touch with a young woman who had given birth to a very sickly baby the month before. Tamiko had hidden her pregnancy and birth from her entire family. She was of Asian descent and knew that her family could never learn of her secret. She had cheated on her husband and felt as though giving birth to a less-than-perfect child was God's way of teaching her a lesson. Tamiko had tried her best to care for this baby but knew that she just could not keep her, and was actually afraid that she might physically harm the baby if she wasn't immediately removed. Her husband left the house and promised not to return until she had gotten rid of the baby. Each time he saw it he became angrier about the affair that had taken place. It was not his baby and he wanted nothing to do with it. The baby had been named Tsi Tsi (Sissy) and barely weighed five pounds. I was told that I needed to find help immediately for this baby, but there was no way that the woman wanted to work with social services. I knew that she would have to work with a social worker eventually, but the most important thing

167

was to get the baby safe. We would hold Tamiko's hand when she did have to go sign papers.

It was only a matter of minutes and I was able to reach one of our Board Members, Bill May, and his wife Patti. They lived just a few miles from where this woman was located. "Hey Billy-Bob. How would you feel about helping save a baby?" He was anxious to help. I explained the whole situation to him and he and Patti offered to transport the baby. Tamiko called the man with whom she had the affair and asked him to pick up the baby. He was given the address of Bill and Patti. As soon as the baby arrived they would head towards my home.

Within two hours little Tsi Tsi was at their door. She arrived in a Mercedes sports car that belonged to her birth father. An older Asian man stepped out of the vehicle and went to the passenger side of the car. His eyes were filled with tears. He had only learned of the fact that he had fathered a baby the week before and was still trying to take it all in. He was married and did not want his family and grown children to be ashamed of what he had done. He would carry this burden alone. He gently lifted the infant seat from the car and sobbed as he walked toward Bill. Bill slowly walked toward the man and offered to take the car seat. "No, I must do this myself," he proclaimed. Bill opened the door to his car and the baby was placed safely in the back where she would remain until she got to her next destination. The man gently kissed his daughter on the forehead for one last time and quietly got back in his car.

Patti sat in the back next to Tsi Tsi while Bill began to drive. We still had no idea where we were going, so I told him to head toward me and if no one else could take her, I would. I had been licensed for high-risk foster children and could do it as a last resort. Fortunately, I had a lot of connections with a lot of other high-risk foster parents and began dialing them in order to find one willing to volunteer to care for Tsi Tsi. As the Mays approached the 405 Freeway, I was able to give them directions where to take the baby. Needless to say, I missed out on taking the kids around the neighborhood that night, but the best treat of all was knowing this

168

little one was safe.

We thought that the most difficult portion of our time with Tsi Tsi was behind us. Not so. There was supposed to be a family interested in adopting her and after they received her medical records, they backed out. The adoption agency had gotten Tsi Tsi's birth parents to sign off, but there was no one who wanted her. We were asked to help search for families that might be willing to adopt.

We went to a doctor with her records and asked for an explanation of her conditions. We learned that besides having a cleft palate she had a heart murmur that would probably require surgery in the near future. This explained why she was always panting. She also had uneven chromosomes which they believed would leave her mentally retarded. The other fear was that she was deaf.

It was not going to be easy, but we would be able to pull this off. We gathered volunteers in my living room, and while children played in the backyard, we began one of our greatest campaigns to find help for someone that I had never even met. We spent three days and hundreds of dollars until we finally got a call that would change this baby's life forever.

A couple by the name of Jemelene and Russ Wilson had been waiting for a second child for almost seven years. They had been called on several other situations, but each time they were called, we were told that this just wasn't their baby. Who was I to question this? I figured it was a "God thing." This time a volunteer called and spoke with Jemelene. She asked the volunteer to give her a few minutes to try and locate her husband. Within five minutes Jemelene called back and told us that she knew this was meant to be her baby

I spoke with Jemelene and went over all the medical information that I knew. I asked if she was certain about this. She told me that she and her husband as well as their daughter Rachel were very excited to adopt this little angel. We were able to get the medical records faxed to the Wilsons and they in turn had them reviewed by

169

their physician while we were getting the records reviewed by a physician in our area. Though there were details included in the papers, it seemed as though there were more questions than answers.

The doctor that the Wilsons spoke with could not give them any clear call on what baby Tsi Tsi's future was going to be like or what the abnormal chromosomes were about. The physician that we spoke with was very negative and in fact told us that he did not think that we would be able to find a family for this baby. Boy, was the doctor surprised when we told him that we had already found a family.

Within days, Russ, Jemelene and Rachel flew down to meet the newest member of their family. They had chosen a name for her. She would be named Allison. Volunteers met them at the airport with signs saying, "Congratulations to the Wilson Family!" and "Welcome Mommy and Daddy...Love Allison!" They loaded in the Cuddle Van and headed towards our home. I got the joy of handing over little Allison to her new family. Both Jemelene and I had tears as she took her new daughter into her arms. "She's so beautiful," she said as she looked into Allison's little almond-shaped eyes. Everyone looked on as rescue baby #175 looked around. I told the Wilsons that I did not believe that their daughter was deaf. Only time would tell.

Emily brought in all her baby doll clothes and handed them over to the family. "Here's what she wears," she stated as she smiled down at the little roommate she had helped nurture. We taught them how to feed Allison with a special nipple for cleft palates. She was so weak because of her heart murmur that she was only able to take a few sips before panting and taking a break. We helped them pack up formula and diapers, and everything else we could find that they might need. They had not had time to put anything together on their own. We took some photos that I still cherish. We got the Wilsons dropped off safely at the hotel. We all slept well that night because we had accomplished what we were told was not possible.

February 3, 2001

I called up to see how Baby Allison was doing. Russ answered the phone. "High Russ, how's she doing?" I asked. Then, I got a weird response back. "Who, Jemelene?" he asked back. I was really thrown off by this question and answered with, "Well, I guess both of them."

Russ said, "Oh, I assumed you had seen the article." What article? What was he talking about? Now my curiosity was really peaked. I was about to learn something so shocking that I was taken back and truly upset by what I heard.

Russ told me that he had sent Jemelene and Allison to Oklahoma for a little R & R. Allison had gone through six operations and Jemelene had been by her side each time. She deserved to take a little time out to see family and friends back in Oklahoma. Jemelene arrived at her cousin's home on January 28, 2001. They took time the first day to catch up and relax. They decided that the following morning they would go to a craft store in the local community and get some materials in order to make scrapbook pages of their time together.

The following morning Jemelene, Allison and Cousin Penny all loaded into Penny's minivan and started out toward the center of town. They enjoyed an early lunch at a local Mexican restaurant and then headed back to the minivan. They were going to drive the two miles to Hobby Lobby.

Just moments before Jemelene and Penny reached the minivan, there was a collision that took place at the nearby street corner. A man had stolen a Dodge Neon and slammed it head-on into an elderly woman's car. He then got out of the vehicle and ran towards the nearby shopping mall.

Jemelene and Penny walked to the minivan and Jemelene began to buckle Allison's car seatbelt. As she finished latching it, she noticed commotion going on over where Penny was standing. She looked up and saw that a man was grabbing Penny and pulling her out of the van. Jemelene realized that this man was trying to take off with the vehicle and all she could think about was getting her little angel out of the back seat. She frantically reached into the back seat and began to try and get the baby's seatbelt off. At the same time, the man was reaching into the back seat and grabbing at little Allison.

The man did not have time to waste. He could hear the sirens in the background as they began to approach. He had to get out of the area and he had to do it NOW! He turned around and turned on the ignition. He quickly put it into reverse and started to take off. Jemelene was knocked to the ground, as was Penny. As he backed up, Penny felt the tire run over her body. Then, just as quickly as it passed from right to left, it again passed over her as he put the van into drive. Jemelene was knocked to the ground by the door on the other side of the van and was screaming for her daughter as the man sped off. Poor Penny was lying on the ground unable to move. Fortunately an EMT who was off-duty came up and began to assess her injuries. Jemelene was screaming at the top of her lungs for help. Anyone within a block could hear her pleas.

The man was desperate to get out of town and recklessly drove into five different vehicles before the van was finally stopped. Officers rushed to the vehicle with their guns drawn and quickly arrested the man. Another officer looked over the front seat in hopes of finding the car seat with the baby in place. The car seat was no longer on the seat of the van, but turned upside down and on the floorboard of the vehicle. He was fearful of even looking at the baby. He hoped that she was all right. He lifted the seat out and there looking back at him were those beautiful little almond eyes. She looked good. The officer summoned paramedics and she was quickly taken into the hospital. Jemelene lost her voice during the time she was calling for help. She quietly wept as she was reunited with her little angel...a true treat.

Allison's mother, Jemelene, says, "Allison has been an incredible blessing to the whole family. The first ten months of having Allison in our care were by far the most challenging and educational, to say the least. Allison has far exceeded what the so-called experts have predicted for her development. Her cleft palate was repaired although she spent nine days (four in ICU) recovering and fighting through the complications. She is NOT deaf and her murmur is now considered small enough that we will wait until she is older and the procedures are more perfected before having it repaired. Allison is a very happy and charming little one who has the patience of Job and the heart of an angel. She is a miracle that myself, Russ and Rachel all feel very fortunate to have in our lives. We will be forever grateful to the birth family who so unselfishly made the choice to place her, and to the Project Cuddle family for not giving up in finding us and giving us the opportunity to be a witness to this sweet miracle."

Chapter Seven

Sometimes Life is So Cruel

Introduction

Sometimes life takes turns that we cannot control. We have to roll with the punches and accept the cards we have been dealt. This chapter, "Sometimes Life is So Cruel," contains the stories of girls and women who were dealt those cards containing physical and emotional challenges that most of us thankfully have never had to endure.

In each instance we were able to be there for each of them as their situations unfolded. No, they did not all come to the same conclusions, but they are all satisfied with the decisions that they have made. I have been honored with photos of each of the children who were born, and each time I look at them, I can't help but smile. It brings back so many memories of joy, frustration, anxiety and finally, contentment.

But Mama
Says I Have To

Samantha Belcoff called our crisis hotline when she was only fifteen years-old. She had been intimate with her boyfriend for six months, since the age of fourteen. Her parents worked full-time so they never noticed that she wasn't coming home right after school. They lived in a little town in the southern part of Idaho. There wasn't a lot for kids to do out there and many of the younger teens found themselves with boyfriends or girlfriends at a very young age.

Samantha hadn't ever had her period, and no one had actually explained how someone could get pregnant. It wasn't until she was at least five months along that she realized something was wrong. She told her mother that she hadn't felt well and needed to go to the doctor. Samantha's mother was in the room with Samantha and when the doctor checked her over, he asked her if she wanted her mother to leave the room. He thought she might be pregnant and wanted to give her privacy in case she didn't want her mother to know. Because Samantha was oblivious to the fact that she might be pregnant, she said that her mother, Beverly, could stay in the room. The doctor assumed that they had spoken about this possibility.

As he began his exam, he started with her eyes and ears. He kept her mind busy with questions so she wouldn't notice that he was actually examining her. He checked her breasts, her glands and now went onto examine her stomach. He took a stethoscope to it to listen for abdominal sounds, and when doing so heard the heartbeat of a baby…Samantha's baby.

"Does the father know?" the doctor asked as he looked up at Samantha. "My father?" she asked. "No, the baby's father," the doctor stated as he looked back at her and then at her mother as he took the tape measure to her belly. He suddenly realized that Samantha wasn't aware of her condition, nor was her mother. "Are you telling me she's pregnant?!?" Beverly shouted. "You mean, my baby is having a baby?!? Oh no! That's not going to happen!" The doctor stood silent. He never did answer her question. She knew the answer. Samantha was in tears as she realized what was going on. She was scared because her mother was so angry and she was very upset because she would probably be told that the baby had to be aborted. She couldn't believe this was happening to her.

The doctor knew that it wasn't wise to keep them in his office, so he quickly finished up with Samantha and left the room. Beverly fussed at Samantha the entire way out of the office, and then as they got into their car it went on. Beverly wanted to know who the father of the baby was and she wanted to know right that minute.

Samantha had been dating a boy by the name of Drew. He had just turned eighteen the week before Samantha found out she was pregnant. Her parents had met him, but had no idea that they had gotten so close. Beverly demanded that Samantha tell her who was responsible for this.

Samantha held off telling her mother for as long as possible. She finally told her mother that it was Drew. She also told her that she loved Drew and hoped to marry him someday.

Beverly didn't want to hear it. She told Samantha that she had to get an abortion or she would call the police and have him arrested for statutory rape. Drew wasn't a bad guy. In fact, he was a very kind young man who really was responsible. He got straight As in school and was going to have a full scholarship to the university just one town away. He had never been in trouble with the law. He became acquainted with Samantha when he saw her walking home in the snow two winters before. He felt so bad for her and asked her if she would like a ride home. They got to know each other as just friends, but eventually this friendship began to grow. Now they were best friends and lovers.

I think that part of the attraction for Samantha was the fact that he was so intelligent. She was extremely mature for her age and was an A and B student. She planned on graduating early and then heading on for college. She was a very goal-oriented person and she realized that she was able to learn so much from him.

When Samantha called our crisis line, she was beside herself. She did not want to abort this baby. She was already five-and-a-half months pregnant and felt that this was a baby conceived in love. She shared with me her concerns. She wanted us to speak with her mother. It was the only hope she had for saving this baby and her relationship with Drew.

At first, I asked her to find a family member whom she felt she could talk with and whom her mother respected. Samantha said that would be her grandmother, Beverly's mother. Samantha called and set up a meeting. Her grandmother knew something was up, but was willing to wait until the next day when they were scheduled to meet if this is what Samantha wanted.

The meeting took place at a coffee shop in town. Samantha was nervous, but so glad that her grandmother was a part of her life. She got there first. She picked a table off in a corner so that they would have a bit more privacy. She waved to her grandmother as she came in the door. Samantha had butterflies in her stomach as she watched her grandmother walk toward her. "Hi Grandma," she said as she got up from her chair to give her a hug. They both sat down and ordered something to drink. Samantha told her grandmother of her dilemma. She knew that being the matriarch of the family, she would have the best chance of convincing Beverly that this was truly a couple in love and that she should leave the couple alone.

The two left the restaurant and headed towards Samantha's house. Samantha wasn't looking forward to this confrontation, but knew that she couldn't put it off any longer. If she did, she was going to end up at an abortion clinic whether she liked it or not. The two went into the house and found Beverly in the kitchen. She knew why they were there. They weren't about to change her mind. She had plans for this girl. This was being done for her; why didn't they see this? What Beverly didn't seem to understand, was the fact that Samantha was against abortions and wouldn't forgive herself if she went this route.

Beverly spoke with the two of them for the next half-hour. It didn't seem to make much of a difference. At this point, Samantha picked up the phone and called the crisis line. I happened to be the one answering the phone. Once I found out who it was, I asked her how she was doing. She explained what was going on, and asked me if I would speak with her mother. She felt as though this was the last option for help.

I spoke with Beverly for about five minutes. She realized how much this baby meant to Samantha and Drew, but felt that she had no alternative but to turn him into the police. She wanted to prove a point; they shouldn't get away with this. I tried to explain to Beverly how much they cared about each other. I asked her one question that ended up making a very big difference in the future of everyone involved. I asked her, "Do you really want this baby to have a father who's in jail?" It was clear to me that this man might serve time, but once he was out, he and Samantha would be back together. They still planned to marry someday.

Well, Beverly became a grandmother in the next few months. Samantha never had to say "good bye" to Drew, and Drew never had to go to jail. Their lives made many turns for the better.

✧✧ UPDATE ✧✧

It has been over three years since I helped Samantha and rescue baby #71. She just wrote me recently and shared with me what had been going on in her life. Samantha actually graduated from high school at the age of 16. She is now in college. She and Drew are still together; in fact they are engaged and will be married before the printing of this book. Their son was born safely and is now almost three years old. Drew was there at the delivery and helped in coaching Samantha. A far cry from the cold cell that he had been headed for. Samantha wrote in her letter, "Thank you for being my son's angel." I had no idea that what I said to her mother would have such an impact. I am so proud of Samantha and what she has accomplished. I hope that others will look to Samantha and strive to turn a challenge into a learning experience.

Pregnant and Living with AIDS

I got a call from a girl named Tiffany in September of 1997. She was being kicked out by her parents and needed a lot of help. She was twenty-four years old and had been on her own off and on since she was sixteen. When I asked her if she was working, she told me that she was a prostitute. She had been doing this for years. There was only one problem—no, actually two problems now.

The first problem was the fact that she had AIDS. She had just discovered this in the past two months. Now, in all good conscience, she couldn't turn tricks for fear of giving them this death sentence as well. She had no idea who the man was who gave it to her, but she had enough sense to not repeat his mistake.

The second problem was that she was pregnant. She found out about her pregnancy when they took her blood. Shortly thereafter she discovered the AIDS situation. She got sick to her stomach when she heard the news. She knew she had been careless and now she was sentenced to death. They had immediately put her on ATZ (a treatment used for patients suffering from HIV) that they hoped would slow down the disease, but the drug was still considered experimental.

I began to ask Tiffany questions about the pregnancy. I found out that she was six months along and had no intentions of keeping this baby. She told me that she had only slept with black men so it would be half African-American and half Native American. Well, this was going to make for an interesting challenge. I couldn't think of too many people right off the top of my head who would want to adopt a baby who was exposed to the AIDS virus, were willing to help care for the birthmother until she delivered, and was of Native American ancestry. No, this was definitely a new one for me.

I knew that shelter was the most important thing for us to work on at this time and so I focused on that first. She lived in the state of Maryland and I began by looking into families in that area. I located two that I would contact immediately. The first was a couple that only wanted to help in sheltering a girl for a week. I asked them if they would consider taking her for a little bit longer, but this wasn't possible. The next couple I called said that they would be willing to take her in. They were actually foster parents and had a lull in cases. They sounded very nice and were willing to meet with the girl immediately.

I called Tiffany and let her know what I had found out. She was so happy to hear the news. They arranged a meeting for the following day. I wished them both good luck and waited to hear what the outcome of this visit would be.

Tiffany and Billy and Cassidy Whitecloud met. It turned out that they really hit it off. I was so pleased to hear this. I didn't even mention the fact that Tiffany was looking to find a family for this baby. I hoped that if they met, things would just work out naturally if it was meant to be.

Sure enough, I got a call about a week after Tiffany moved in with the Whiteclouds. David Whitecloud was on one phone and Tiffany was on the extension. They both asked questions about the possibility of letting the Whiteclouds adopt this baby. I told them that they should contact an attorney in their area and try to discuss it with him. I thought that since they were both Native American the chances would be much greater.

I didn't hear from the Whiteclouds or from Tiffany for almost a

184

month. I left messages, but I just had to assume everything was all right. If something was wrong, I was sure we would have heard from them. When I did finally get a call back, they informed me that everything was going great. Tiffany had spoken with her parents and they said that she could come back home and they would take care of her if she didn't bring the baby with her. Tiffany had decided that she would let them pamper her a bit. She left the world of prostitution and was going to look into going to college.

Cassidy took Tiffany for her next doctor's visit. She was now 39 weeks along. Cassidy heard the baby's heart beat and watched as Tiffany's belly moved up and down. A C-section was scheduled and Tiffany asked Cassidy to be her coach. Cassidy was thrilled at the thought. It would be a real joy for her to get to be the first one to see the new baby. They knew it was going to be a boy, but hadn't chosen a name at this point. With a date scheduled they now needed to get started on making some choices.

Finally, on December 15th Tiffany went into the hospital and was prepared for surgery. Through her IV, she was given an extra large dose of ATZ right before surgery. Cassidy went in and got gowned up. Billy went into the waiting room and paced until he heard those wonderful words: "Congratulations…you have a new son!" Cassidy took her husband over to see the newest member of the Whitecloud family, rescue baby #98.

✧✧ UPDATE ✧✧

Well, the Whitecloud family is doing great! Their son tested negative for HIV and is growing like a weed. They have heard a couple of times from Tiffany. She is still hanging in there. She took a couple of night courses, but isn't strong enough to work. She has gotten closer to her parents than ever before.

The Whiteclouds are now expecting another child in their family. It is a situation very similar to the first. This time it will be a little girl. They are glad that they can complete their family and help a couple of women who felt so hopeless.

My Baby Won't Grow!

May 4, 1998

Tanya Brown had two little boys that she had given birth to illegitimately. Her parents had supported her during the first pregnancy, but when she became pregnant with the second one at the age of seventeen they made her leave. Eventually, they fell in love with the second son she delivered and treated him just as well as the first son. Tanya loved both her sons and was doing her best to try and raise them by herself.

She rented a bedroom from a little old lady in Philadelphia, PA. Fortunately for Tanya she rented the bedroom from someone who was hard of hearing. This little old lady was named Lilly. She had been a widow for almost thirty years and was happy to have some young blood in her home. She would watch the two boys when Tanya went to work. The boys were one and three years old. Though they were quite a handful they never seemed to bother Lilly.

Tanya's parents only saw her once or twice a year. They were still upset with her for having little Jimmy. "Too many mistakes," her mama said. Tanya knew she was right, but she couldn't go through an abortion and she knew it was her responsibility, so she kept Jimmy.

Tanya was working as a full-time dental assistant in a very nice dental office. She had worked her way up to the position of office manager. She was good at what she did, but seemed to be having a difficult time concentrating lately. She couldn't put her finger on exactly what the problem was and so she just ignored it.

August 14, 1998

Tanya's mother was celebrating her 60th birthday and Tanya would be expected to attend. She'd been saving for a long time in order to buy a special gift for the occasion. She had picked out a beautiful cherry wood jewelry box. The cost was $58, but she thought that her mother would be impressed by it.

Tanya and the boys arrived at her mother's house on time. Her mother opened the front door and took one look at Tanya and then said, "Girl, you did it again, didn't you?" Tanya didn't know what her mother was talking about. "You're pregnant aren't you?" her Mama stated. "Mama, don't be crazy, I am nothing of the sort!" Tanya proclaimed. She handed her mother her birthday gift and walked on into the house with her two boys following behind.

The evening went well and Tanya's gift went over wonderfully. Her mother actually got tears in her eyes when she opened the gift. She was very proud of her daughter and what she had accomplished.

September 25, 1998

Tanya had been losing weight and was extremely tired. She was afraid to go to the doctor. She thought that she might have cancer or a brain tumor. She figured that if she didn't go she could avoid what they were going to tell her. What she didn't know wouldn't hurt her.

October 26, 1998

Tanya was too exhausted to even go to work. Her feet were swelling and she had a terrible headache that had not gone away for over three days. She asked Lilly to watch the children and she begged her girlfriend Linda to take her to the emergency room. Something was really wrong and she couldn't ignore it any longer.

When she got to the emergency room they checked Tanya in and took her vitals. She hated needles. She knew that they would probably take some blood and right now she felt so bad that she didn't even care what they did to her.

The physician asked Tanya a lot of questions and gave her a basic exam before blood work was taken. There was an hour of waiting time before they got the results back. When the doctor came back to see her, he had another doctor along with him. Her name was Dr. Noelle Lewis. Tanya was really getting worried now. Dr. Lewis explained that they had some of the preliminary test results back and that she had severe toxemia and her blood pressure was sky high. She didn't understand a lot of what the doctor was saying, but did understand the part about doing an ultrasound.

An IV was started and Tanya was wheeled into the ultrasound area. Once the technician applied gel to Tanya's tiny tummy the technician began to search within for answers to what Tanya's problem was. "Oh wow, it's bigger than I suspected," the technician said. Tanya could feel herself getting flushed. Her head was killing her so she really couldn't concentrate very well. She began to think that maybe she would be better off if she were dead.

After the ultrasound was completed Tanya was wheeled back to her cubicle where Linda had been waiting. Dr. Lewis immediately came in with a concerned look on her face. She held Tanya's hand and proceeded to gently try and explain what was going on. "Tanya, your blood pressure is very high. We've put you on medication that will bring it down. Your headache should begin to go away. Now, we did an ultrasound and we're worried about the baby." Tanya's eyes had been shut because of the bright lights until that moment. "Baby!?! What baby?" she questioned.

Dr. Lewis explained that she was approximately seven months pregnant, but the baby was very small for its gestational age. She knew that most of the information she was giving Tanya was probably going in one ear and out the other. The doctor would explain each detail to Tanya, but look at Linda as well. She hoped that this young woman would be able to help Tanya out with the details once she left the E.R.

Tanya was admitted to the obstetric floor. She remained there for the next three days. Miss Lilly had the boys, so she didn't have to worry. Her headache had completely disappeared by the time she was dismissed. She felt that she was not going to be able to keep this baby and she did not want her parents to ever find out about it. Linda had heard about Project Cuddle and suggested that Tanya should call for help. She was glad to give it a try, but really had no idea what she was going to do. She was so afraid that if she tried to give up this baby, they would take away the other two. She wasn't about to let that happen. She wasn't at all attached to this baby, so it seemed harder for her to come up with any real plan of action.

That's when I got the call. Tanya told me about her situation and how scared she was. She would go home to her little room in little Miss Lilly's house and care for her two sons. She could barely deal with the cards she had just been dealt.

October 30, 1998

It was almost noon when I got another call from Tanya. She was feeling much better and wanted to talk about what to do with this baby. I shared with her all the different options. She told me that unless she found out that she couldn't have any other children and this was a girl, she was definitely giving it up. She decided that she wanted to come out to visit me in California. She wasn't going to make a decision with her sons running all over the place. She wanted some time to clear her head. We checked with her doctor who felt that Tanya was doing better and it would be all right for her to take the trip.

November 23, 1998

She came out on the Amtrak and stayed with our family. After being with us for a week, Tanya began to have headaches. I took her to a local obstetrician to get checked out. I was worried about how she looked. I noticed her feet were beginning to swell even though we had kept her off of salts and away from sodas.

The obstetrician seemed unusually serious as he studied the measurements of Tanya's belly and took her vitals. He gave me a prescription for an emergency ultrasound. We went next door to get this test done. Once we had finished, we were told to return to the obstetrician's office.

We were escorted into the private office of Dr. Sanders this time instead of an exam room. I knew something bad was up, but I wasn't sure what he was going to say. I hoped the baby was all right. We wouldn't have to wait long before we found out what was going on.

The doctor sat down and showed us a copy of the ultrasound. She began to explain that the baby was suffering from In Utero Growth Retardation. For some reason the baby was not getting the nutrients that were needed in order for it to grow. It could be due partially because of her high blood pressure. The doctor put Tanya on complete bed rest and she was to drink Ensure between meals.

I would like to say that Tanya was a pleasant patient. This was partially true. She did have a few good days, but for the most part, she wasn't very happy. She was frustrated by her physical limitations and resented the fact that she couldn't be open with her mother. I tried to encourage Tanya to speak with her mom; she still avoided it at all costs. She missed her sons so much, but knew that she had to stay put until after she delivered.

November 30, 1998

I took Tanya back to the doctor's for a non-stress test. She was not doing well at all and my guess was that they would admit her to the hospital. Sure enough, the doctor took one look at her and instructed the nurse to take Tanya's blood pressure. It was sky high and she was immediately wheeled over to the maternity ward at the hospital. Fortunately, it was only a "stone's throw away."

It appeared on the ultrasound that the baby still was not growing as it should. They were very concerned that this child might not survive in the womb much longer. They were also concerned that Tanya would not survive this pregnancy. A high-risk obstetrician was called in for a consultation. Tanya was immediately admitted to the hospital where she would remain for the rest of her pregnancy.

December 6, 1998

When I came into Tanya's hospital room that day, she looked terrible. She had her hands over her eyes. The bright light was really bothering her. Her face seemed swelled to twice the size that it was normally. I went to the nurse's station and asked them to page the doctor. Tonya's nurse was very sweet and got in touch with Dr. Lewis right away. Fortunately, she was in the building finishing up a delivery. It only took about twenty minutes before she was by Tonya's bed. One look and she knew why I had asked for her to be paged. Dr. Lewis contacted the high-risk obstetrician who was on call. They both agreed that it was time for an emergency C-section. It was scheduled within an hour of their meeting. The doctors weren't at all happy with the size of the baby, but they knew that Tanya would surely die if the baby were not delivered right away. They had given steroids to Tanya in the past, so hopefully the baby's lungs would be developed enough that it could fight to stay alive.

"It's a girl!!!" Dr. Lewis exclaimed. The nurses were all so excited to finally meet this little one who had caused Tanya so much trouble. They had made bets on whether or not she would keep the baby. The majority felt that once she had seen this little one it would touch her heart and she would no longer fear letting the family know about the pregnancy.

It was late in the evening when Tanya woke up enough to know what was going on. I was sitting by her side. "Is the baby okay?" she asked in a very quiet voice. I told her that everything was fine. I asked her if she wanted to see the baby. She told me that at this time she didn't want to. She still wasn't sure what she was going to do.

December 7, 1998

Dr. Lewis stopped in to check on Tanya. She sat on the side of her bed and looked her straight in the eyes. "Tanya, I need to tell you something. You are lucky to be alive. Your daughter is doing fine. She's small but very strong." This was the first Tanya knew of the sex of the baby. The doctor continued, "This pregnancy was extremely hard on your poor body. You will not be able to have any other children. I know that you have some decisions to make, and we have a social worker on staff if you would like to speak with her."

What Dr. Lewis just told her changed everything. She had always dreamed of having a daughter. In fact, she and her mother would occasionally daydream together. Knowing that she would never have another chance of having a child changed everything. "No thanks," Tanya said as she smiled up at the doctor. "I know what I'm going to do. Can you please have them bring me my daughter?" Dr. Lewis smiled and quickly left the room. When she returned, she held Tanya's little prize package. "Here she is," the doctor announced. "She weighed in at four pounds, four ounces, but she's doing just fine."

Tanya held rescue baby #55 to her breast and then asked, "What's your first name?" Dr. Lewis looked at her and smiled. "It's Noelle." Tonya said, "I like that. Noelle Lilly Brown. That flows beautifully, and Noelle is perfect for the Christmas season."

✧✧ UPDATE ✧✧

I held Tanya's hand as she called her mother and let her know that she had a granddaughter. Tanya is back living with Miss Lilly and has been given another bedroom at no extra cost. Miss Lilly has really grown attached to Noelle.

Tanya has gotten a scholarship for college. She plans on becoming a dental hygienist. This way, she will be able to work part time and financially support her children, yet spend a lot of time with them as they continue to grow. Tanya's mother has been very understanding and is watching the children at least two evenings a month.

One Lesbian's Secret

Annie had led a tough life. At the very young age of four, she was put into foster care because of sexual abuse by both of her parents. She had been tossed from foster home to foster home for the next fourteen years. She was not lucky when it came to getting into good homes. She suffered mental abuse by some and physical abuse by others. Annie's survival mechanism was to detach herself from the situation. She told me that she was able "…to slip deep within and away." She survived those years and ran away just before she turned eighteen years old.

Years have passed since those horrible nights of abuse, and Annie has successfully gotten her life together. She fell in love with a beautiful woman by the name of Laura. She met Laura one night when she was out shooting pool. Laura spotted Annie the moment she walked into the bar. Annie was actually making a move on Laura's "ex" when Laura found herself walking over to join the conversation. It did not take long and they were deep in a conversation about baseball. One thing led to another and in a matter of days they became good friends, and eventually lovers.

August 7, 2000

One cold winter evening, Annie took Laura to work just as she always had. They did not have enough money for an apartment at that time, and so Annie would sleep in the car at night on Laura's job site and then Laura would sleep in a back room while Annie was working during the day. This particular evening Laura had gone into work at the strip club like any other night. She had worked there for over three years and knew everyone on the payroll. They knew that Annie was sleeping in the parking lot and sometimes the bartender would bring out some "munchies" for her.

Annie ate the snacks that had been brought to her that evening and then put her coat behind her head as she turned it into a make-shift pillow. It had been an extremely long day and Annie nodded off to sleep within a matter of moments. The wind was howling and tumbleweeds would hit the car every once in a while, but Annie didn't even hear them. She was "dead to the world."

Suddenly, Annie was jolted awake. She couldn't figure out exactly what was going on, but could smell liquor and hear a man's voice as she was being grabbed. She was violently dragged out of her car and pushed down onto the asphalt. He continued to squeeze her throat as he told her to keep quiet. Annie found herself disappearing into an "out of body" experience just as she had when she was being abused as a child. She had no idea who this man was, but prayed that he wouldn't kill her.

After what seemed like hours, the man slithered away into the night just as quickly as he had appeared. Annie waited until she was sure that he was gone and then got up and readjusted her clothes as she climbed back into the car. She made certain that she locked the doors this time and then went back to sleep while she waited for Laura.

Nothing was ever said by Annie about what went on that night. Annie never planned on letting anyone know. What was the point? "It wasn't like they could do anything about it," Annie later said.

October 2, 2000

Annie was worried. She missed her period. That was unheard of for her. She knew she was pregnant, but still wanted to confirm it with a pregnancy test. She went to the local market to purchase a pregnancy test and found that she was too ashamed to let anyone see what she buying, so she just took it. She was so angry with God when she saw the results. How could He let her get into this mess? She'd been through so much during her short lifetime and

196

she didn't deserve this. She just could not bring herself to tell Laura. She finally had someone in her life that she cared about and who cared about her. She was afraid that Laura would not look at her in the same way ever again. Annie decided that she would take care of it by drinking in excess. Maybe she could "drink it to death." She would punch her stomach with the hopes that this might jar it loose. She had nothing to lose and everything to gain.

December 10, 2001

Laura was beginning to question Annie about why she had been so grouchy. She could tell something was wrong, but she couldn't put her finger on it. Laura was always told that everything was fine. Annie had always been the "butch," (the strong one in the relationship), but her hormones were beginning to play tricks on her. She would look forward to those few minutes of time alone in a shower so that she could cry without the fear of being heard.

Christmas Day

The Christmas tree lights had been plugged in all night. When Laura woke up that Christmas morning, she anxiously went into the living room and waited to see the expression on Annie's face when she entered the room. She was so grateful for all the work that Annie had done over the past few months. Sure, Laura was still stripping and doing her share to pay the bills, but Annie had worked on weekends and financially helped them get an apartment. For the first time they were going to be able to celebrate as a "couple" with a roof over their heads instead of in their car.

By ten o'clock in the morning Annie finally dragged herself out of bed. Laura could hear that Annie had gotten sick in the bathroom. "Are you alright, Sweetie?" Laura asked as she tapped on the bathroom door. Annie reassured her that she was fine and then came out to face Laura. She didn't dare tell her today. She still planned on getting an abortion since the drinking binges did not work. She had found a clinic in the yellow pages that would do abortions up to 24 weeks. She'd take her vacation money to pay for it. She thought why should she traumatize Laura when she could simply take care of it herself.

Laura and Annie sat on the floor next to the Christmas tree and began to open the gifts they had gotten for each other. Levina was thrilled with her gift certificate for sessions at the local tanning salon. She also received a beautiful sterling silver necklace with a locket that was intricately carved.

Annie's gifts started off practical. The first was a jigsaw that she had been asking for. The second was a personalized license plate. Annie was having a hard time holding back the tears with this gift. The final gift was a beautiful blue bowling ball with her name engraved on it. When Annie saw this, she went into tears.

This threw Laura completely off. She had suspected what might be wrong with Annie, but that just did not make any sense at all. She knew that Annie would never cheat on her, so she could not possibly be pregnant...right? She held onto Annie and finally asked, "Babe, are you pregnant?"

Annie quickly pulled away with a major look of shock on her face. She could not believe that Laura had figured out what her secret was. "How did you find out?" she asked. This in turn threw Laura into shock. "Oh my God...you are?" she exclaimed. "How? Who? Why?"

Annie went on to explain what had happened and how she had just blocked it out of her mind. Laura could not handle the thought that Annie had gone through this all by herself. As she held this tough, masculine, strong woman, her heart began to melt. She told Annie that she was willing to stand by her side and help her in raising this little one.

January 9, 2001

Time was running out for Annie to seek an abortion. She still was not convinced that she could handle it any other way. This particular Tuesday Laura had her tanning appointment scheduled at 9:30 a.m. She promised that she would take Annie to the clinic after getting some tanning time in. While walking into the tanning salon, Laura noticed a display of small business-like cards on the counter. The information read "Project Cuddle is a 24 hour confidential crisis hotline helping to provide women with alternatives to abandoning their newborn babies." Laura took the card and called Project Cuddle from a pay phone before returning home.

Angel took the call that day when Laura called. Angel explained that we wanted to speak with her partner if she could get her to the phone. Laura explained that she really wanted to help Annie in raising this baby and she hoped that we could offer her some help. Annie was feeling so guilty about drinking and abusing herself that she was afraid that the baby would be permanently damaged. We explained that we would get her to a doctor in order to see how she and the baby were doing. Perhaps she could find out enough information that it would make her decision a bit easier.

January 10, 2001

Annie was too frightened to talk with anyone on the phone, so we arranged for Angel and my daughter Lani to meet with both Annie and Laura for dinner at a local restaurant. Laura and Annie were late and so Lani and Angel played checkers in the lobby for about half an hour. Angel got a call on her cell phone from the Project Cuddle operator on call. It was a message from Laura. They were on their way but running late due to traffic, so Lani and Angel decided to go on in and sit down to wait.

Angel was able to see everyone who was coming into the restaurant from where she was. Finally, she saw Laura. She had long blonde hair, and was tan and petite. Next to her was Annie. Her head hung down and she wore a baseball cap to hide herself from eye contact. She wore an oversized flannel shirt with jeans. Angel waved them over to their table where she introduced herself and Lani. Throughout the meal Annie stayed quiet and either looked down or at Laura. Eye contact was very limited. Angel was able to get a little bit of information out of Annie, but it was basically like pulling teeth. She began to open up a bit as the meal came to an end.

As they said their goodbyes, Laura gave Angel and Lani a hug. Annie was another story. Angel ended up saying, "Okay, time for a hug," as she gently embraced Annie. There was a tear in Annie's eye as Angel reassured her that everything was going to be fine and she'd call her first thing in the morning with the name and phone number of a doctor who would see her. Annie realized that no one was going to hurt her and she was going to get help.

January 12, 2001

Most obstetricians will not take a woman's case if she is more than three or four months pregnant. We have one wonderful doctor by the name of Dr. Jan who will help us with girls who are further along, and sometimes about to deliver. Angel called and spoke to the nurse regarding a young woman who would be calling for an appointment. Laura made an appointment and she went with Annie for support. Both Annie and the baby looked good. Laura and Annie had made a decision that they both agreed upon. They were going to give this baby a chance at life and raise it together. Annie did not care if it was a boy or a girl she was just thrilled that Laura was going to stand by her and that the baby was all right. The guilt that she felt still haunted her.

April 29, 2001

Over the next few months, Angel became very close to Laura and Annie. She watched Annie turn into a woman who was willing to accept this baby that she carried within. When times got tough, Angel was there by her side. When Annie went to the doctor's office to find out if it was a boy or a girl, Angel was the first one Annie called to share the news with.

Early that Sunday morning, Angel got the call from Laura that she had been waiting for. "We need you now! Annie is in labor and we need a ride to the hospital!" Laura was way too nervous to drive. With the keys to the Cuddle Van, Angel was on her way to experience the birth of baby number 350. Two hours of pushing and finally a beautiful little girl arrived. Angel held little Georgia

Jewell while Laura wiped Annie's brow. A situation that seemed so hopeless just a few months ago looked completely different as they all gazed down on this new little life. No, this was not a traditional family, but a family filled with love and a baby with a future.

Chapter Eight

Hope for the Future

Introduction

When I began to write this chapter, "Hope for the Future," I wasn't sure where to start. I know that you're now very aware of the fact that there are a lot of girls out there who have pregnancies they neither want nor accept. They hide their pregnancies and then abandon the baby upon birth. The good news is that there is hope. Each tiny little life and every girl who finds herself in this situation deserve to have a bright ending available. There are others in the country who are making a difference as well. The following are a few of their stories.

Little Miss Gigi

Easter 1999

It was Easter Sunday and Gigi Kelly and her family decided that they would go and visit her mother's church for the sunrise service. It was expected to be a wonderful celebration. All the children were going to be singing in the service and Gigi's little daughter would be part of this spectacular event. As they pulled in they could see red and blue flashing lights reflecting off the church building.

Police were blocking off the area on the far side of the sanctuary. Gigi's husband parked the car and the entire family exited. Gigi's heart began beating faster. "Hold on kids!" she shouted as they ran on ahead to the crime scene. It was too late. They were already way ahead of her. She just hoped that there wasn't anything that they would be seeing that could upset them.

As Gigi got up to the sight, she noticed a small yellow line that had been sprayed on the ground. It wasn't in the shape of anything in particular, but this seemed to be the center of the focus of all the investigators. She looked up and saw the pastor over to the right of the crowd and decided that she would go on over and ask him what had happened.

Gigi was shocked by what she heard. Late that Saturday evening, two teens who were out on a walk heard a noise coming from the church. They decided to investigate. They thought it might be an abandoned kitten or injured puppy. They ran to the top of the hill; only to find that the sound they had heard was getting fainter.

They were afraid they might be too late. There, between the church's outside wall and a pine tree lay a blanket in disarray. The teens stopped dead in their tracks when off to the side of the blanket they saw a quiver of movement from what appeared to be a doll. Then they heard another sound, like those they heard on their way up the hill. "Oh my God, it's a baby!" one teen shouted. They scooped the little baby up and placed it in a windbreaker that the second teen was wearing and then called for help.

The poor little baby was sunburned and filthy from being in the dirt. She remained that way until after she arrived at the hospital where she was quickly examined. The doctor estimated she was almost a day old when her tiny naked body was dropped off at the church. She was given the name "Baby June" by the hospital staff. Gigi, a nurse and mother, learned how lucky "Baby June" was and realized that she needed to do something to make sure this never happened again.

Gigi contacted her local media and told them of the assistance she was offering. She called it "Baskets for Babies." (She now had placed an old laundry basket filled with soft, fresh blankets on her front porch.) The neighbors and community around her rallied together and within a matter of months she had hundreds of baskets on front porches just like hers. She would now sleep easier at night knowing that she had at least let the immediate area know of her concern and she hoped that any girl contemplating such an act would seek out hers or another volunteer's basket instead of a trash can.

Gigi continued these efforts and her total reached over 600 families that participated in this program. She eventually had her basket on "Oprah" to share her program, and that is when I first heard about her. Since that time, Gigi has joined Project Cuddle's forces. We now work with her volunteers and when a girl in the Pennsylvania area needs help, we call on some of Gigi's supporters. In fact, Gigi recently helped with a case in her area. Now, volunteers keep their baskets out and their doors open to helping any girl or woman who is in need. When Project Cuddle calls, these great volunteers really make a difference. Gigi said it best: "We can't keep following dead babies' coffins. We've got to do something to protect these little ones." Together we are and that is exciting.

Baby Saver
East

April 19, 2000

I had just finished taping a live episode of "OPRAH." The
driver was taking us back to the train station as I got a call from
Elizabeth McKibbin. She was one of the hotline operators who had
been on call that morning. She was so excited when she called.
"Debbe, you have to call this guy. He's great! He's been looking
for you for two years. You've got to call him. He buries babies
and saves them too, but in the New York area. He says he'll even
fly out here to meet you!" I could not understand her excitement,
but I promised Elizabeth that I would give him a call when I got
back to town.

Two weeks passed by and I was finally able to find the time to
give Mr. Jaccard a call. Elizabeth was right. I not only met a great
guy, but the eastern version of me. He told me about a few of the
situations he worked with and he amazed me. Timothy is very ani-
mated and I truly enjoy listening to his thick New York accent as
he shares each story. He told me about the time he was holding a
funeral for a little baby by the name of Christina Hope. Hope is
always the last name of babies that Timothy and the AMT Children
of Hope Foundation Infant Burial, Inc., bury. The funeral was being held in Manhattan at St. Patrick's Cathedral. The officers were
there in full uniform and the hearse was pulled up to the front of the
church. The front door to the cathedral was locked. The priest was
new, and unaware of how things were normally carried out. When
Timothy was unable to convince the priest that he should open
those front doors Timothy decided to take things into his own
hands. Timothy believed that the baby's casket should be brought

209

down the center aisle of the church and be allowed the respect that she deserved but never got while alive.

Timothy wasn't about to allow this priest to change his plans. This was one of his Hope Children. She would get the respect in death that she never got in her very brief but profound life. Timothy found a way to get the front doors open to the sanctuary. Baby Christina Hope was slowly carried in her tiny casket down the red carpet. Many tears were shed that day. Prayers were said for both Baby Christina and the woman who left her in a dumpster in a back alley off Broadway and 7th Avenue.

Timothy shared his message with the congregation. He let them know that each baby was named with the last name of Hope so that through their deaths, perhaps there was hope that others could take advantage of his help and the help of others in the community. Those who attended that day all walked away with the knowledge that this baby was now in a resting place with over twenty other little Hope Children. She would never blow bubbles, have a 1st birthday or be carried on her Daddy's shoulders, but she would always be loved, and now she would be held in Heaven by all the angels.

He told me about one of his most recent crisis situations. He had gotten a call from a very frightened girl in the Bronx. She told Timothy that she had her one-month-old baby and didn't want him any longer. She had never really wanted him but was trying to keep him for the sake of her family. It wasn't fifteen minutes after this call came in that Timothy was on his way to rescue this baby. He followed the instructions that she had given him over the phone.

The baby was going to be left on the last subway car. She would then get off when they got to the subway station. Once she left the subway, he would open the door to the adjoining subway car and pick up the baby. Then he would proceed to the nearest hospital.

Things did not go as planned. She placed the baby in the back car and on the seat, just as she said she would. Timothy tried to open the door to this subway car and couldn't get it to open. It was actually locked. He saw two young men looking at the baby who was lying there on the bench by itself. He realized that they were about to pick the baby up. He rushed out of the subway car as the two men began running up the stairs. The taller one had the little bundle in his arms as they headed towards the downtown area of the city. Timothy had to try and catch these guys. He didn't know what they were going to do but he could only hope that they wouldn't hurt the baby.

Timothy hollered to try and get their attention, but there was so much noise on the city streets that only those he was running by could hear his yells. He could tell that they were going in the direction of the hospital. This made him feel a bit better, but he had promised this girl that he wouldn't get this baby involved with social services until they had spoken the following day. He was hoping that she just needed a little break and would change her mind in the morning. If the baby got into the system, it wasn't going to be so easy to get the baby back.

Timothy was able to catch the two men as they got to the foot of the hospital steps. He showed them his AMT badge and was able to explain what was going on. Eventually, this young lady got her life in order and we are happy to say that she is now raising her precious son. Timothy was instrumental in pushing for the Baby Abandonment Bill in New York.

✧✧ UPDATE ✧✧

Timothy's efforts temporarily shifted due to the bombing of the World Trade Center. He has been assisting with the morgue detail and will hopefully be able to help New York return to normal in the near future.

Now What?

September 1999

A new law was passed in the state of Texas. It was called the "Abandoned Baby Bill"[1] and was designed to stop a rash of abandonments that had taken place: "In Houston, residents recently discovered that they had an epidemic on their hands: Over a 10 month period, 13 newborn babies were found in trashcans, front porches, or by the side of the road. Three of them were found dead. It got so bad that the city had to put up billboards telling women not to chuck their babies."[2] Nationwide media shared the story of Houston and how they were the first to pass such a law. The hope of some Texans was that this new law would stop any further incidents.

A man by the name of George Ford, a social worker for the Houston area, had spent many years helping the less fortunate. Though he was not personally involved with the law and it's passing, he was now being given instructions to help implement it. I first met George in February of 2000. I was asked to come out to Houston by an NBC producer to discuss my concerns on the show "Dateline NBC LIVE" in Houston. George and I shared the stage that day.

"The rash of incidents spurred the formation of the Task Force on Baby Abandonment."[3] The following day I met George along with many wonderful local officials and lay people on this task force. I learned that their hearts were in the right place and they had high hopes that a crisis phone line would be manned by social services that would be able to stop abandonment all together.

Many states have followed Texas in passing such laws. Laws tend to vary in every state. Most tend to give a birthmother an "Affirmative Defense." No, this does not mean that they are automatically dismissed of charges if they bring a baby safely into a hospital. Justin Unruh, spokesman for state Rep. Geanie Morrison, said, "The law does not guarantee that a parent will not be prosecuted for child abandonment. That decision," he said, "is up to the prosecutor."[4] What it means is that it gives the mother or father a positive defense if they are prosecuted. The state of California, with the help of Senator James Brulte and Assemblyman Ken Maddux, pushed through a law that allows a mother complete immunity from prosecution if the baby is delivered within 72 hours of its birth and is in healthy condition. This was a needed improvement in the law.

Some states allow for a mother to deliver a baby to a hospital and abandon it up to 30 days after birth, and others allow this to take place up to only 72 hours after birth. Some states only allow hospital medical staff to receive newborns while in others the law allows anyone to be considered a "safe haven recipient."

I am often asked how I feel about these laws. To be honest, I feel very uncomfortable. Until these past few weeks, I could not quite put my finger on it. The laws were made to save lives. According to an article in the New York Times dated August 31, 2001, "Of the first 16 states that passed the laws, only six reported safe haven babies in a survey by the National Conference of State Legislatures. And babies continue to be abandoned illegally in states with the laws—more frequently, in some cases, than in states without them."[5] I know personally of at least five cases where the baby would most have certainly died if medical treatment had not been administered at the last minute. Prenatal care, responsibility, and accountability can all be achieved. Let me share with you one of Project Cuddle's situations.

April 2001

It has been four months since California passed the law that would allow a woman to abandon her newborn at a hospital with no questions asked. When this particular call came in, I was informed that there was a young woman who was almost nine months pregnant with no prenatal care and using cocaine and heroine (speed balls) on a daily basis. She did not want to get arrested by deliver-

214

ing a drug-exposed baby at the hospital or lose custody of her two other children when her past history was revealed. This woman, we'll call her Sophie, had gotten pregnant while working as a prostitute. She had no idea who the father was or even what race this child would be.

My daughter-in-law Talea worked on getting a volunteer assigned to this case. A wonderful volunteer by the name of Crystal Martell was ready to do whatever she could to make sure that both Sophie and the baby would be fine. We were able to convince Sophie that she could safely deliver in a hospital and then if she chose, give the baby up without fear of her other children being taken away. We were able to get her prenatal care, emotional support and make sure that if she tested HIV positive she could get the proper care immediately.

Well, it worked, and thank God it did. She delivered that following week. We had time to get her HIV testing done and fortunately it came back negative. Another volunteer by the name of Lynn Dupre was at Sophie's side as she delivered. The baby had a bowel movement in the birth canal and was in great danger of inhaling the dark, tar-like mixture called meconium when it took it's first breath. During labor the NICU nurse was brought down to the delivery room and the baby was safely delivered without complications. If Sophie had delivered at home the chances of this baby surviving would have been very slim. We were told by the medical staff that the baby most likely would have died if it had not received medical treatment immediately. Sophie had planned on keeping the baby at home for a day before having a friend drop the baby off. By then, the baby would most likely have been dead or near death. With our efforts this did not happen, and rescue baby #340 was saved.

Another situation that we recently ran into occurred when Angel spoke with a young woman on the crisis line the other day who had called an adoption agency for help. She was married, but separated and did not want the baby. She was afraid that if she told her husband about the pregnancy, he would beat her up. She wanted the agency to help her in finding an adoptive family. Here are the options that the agency gave her:

#1. Be legally divorced 300 days before the baby is born. (impossible)
#2. Pray that he gets hit by a bus.
#3. Abandon the baby at a hospital...it's legal now.

None of these were suitable answers for her. We were able to get her a local volunteer for support, as well as legal assistance that she needed in order to get through this situation.

October 2000

I attended a symposium hosted by the Child Welfare League of America in Washington, D.C. I met a wonderful woman by the name of Maureen Hogan. Maureen has adopted three children in the past ten years. Two of those children were abandoned at birth and suffered going through foster home after foster home over the next several years. By the time that they were eligible for adoption, their options were not great. There just weren't nearly enough qualified homes willing to adopt older children. Fortunately, for these particular children, they met Maureen and her husband.

When the issue of the baby abandonment came to the surface, Maureen started to realize that there were many points of concern. She told me about one young woman by the name of Mimi who found herself pregnant at the age of 15. Mimi had heard about the new law in Texas and planned all along on using it. Unfortunately, Mimi went into a coma when she was six and a half months along. Her family had no idea what was wrong with their daughter since they were not aware of her pregnancy. Mimi was rushed to the nearest hospital where the doctors discovered her blood pressure was dangerously high. They discovered the pregnancy and explained the danger that their daughter and the baby were currently dealing with. Mimi's parents had no real option but to authorize an emergency C-section with the hopes of saving both of their lives. The tiny baby boy was put immediately on life support. Mimi remained in a coma for a week. When she finally woke up, her family asked her why she never told them that she was pregnant. She told them that she planned all along to use the baby abandonment law to drop the baby off at a hospital when it was born. Unfortunately, because Mimi had to deliver so early, the baby is now a vegetable and is considered unadoptable. If this girl had gotten prenatal care this could have been avoided completely. My heart ached when Maureen told me this story.

Maureen introduced me to a man by the name of Ron Morgan, the Executive Director of Bastard Nation (BN). Adults who discovered they had no family history put this organization together. Most members had sealed records that they would never be able to get to. Ron had no idea that he had been adopted until after both his parents passed away. He was 36 years old at the time. He was going through some personal papers in the attic when he came across papers that showed the secret that his parents had kept from him all his life. He was adopted. Ron began a journey to discover what being adopted meant, both personally and culturally. This journey lead him to join BN and eventually he was invited to join the leadership team. In 2000, as "Safe Haven" laws began to pop up in state legislation all over the country, Ron led the team to analyze and create the BN position paper on these new laws. Ron and his organization had concerns about the ramifications of implementing baby abandonment laws. People who dropped children off at the hospital doors most likely would not be giving medical information or histories of either parent. They would end up much like Ron with secret pasts and no way of finding out the truth.

So as you have seen, there is no clear-cut solution to this problem. There is no right or wrong. If the laws save babies, that is great. If we loose some because of no prenatal care or safe hospital delivery, then we may need to adjust these laws.

An exciting new step in the larger picture of baby abandonment is that we are now working with the state of Colorado to help them with public awareness. The goal is to educate students at all schools throughout the state about Project Cuddle's toll-free number. The law was passed over a year ago and yet, no person has taken advantage of it with success. Unfortunately, four babies suffered the tragic fate of abandonment after its implementation. The good news is that during that same period of time Project Cuddle was able to rescue four babies in the state of Colorado. I met a wonderful woman by the name of Janet Motz from the Department of Colorado Social Services while at the symposium in Washington D.C. She has successfully help lead the way in making it possible for the private sector and social services to work together. We are working together to launch a public awareness campaign throughout the state. Those who call the crisis line from this particular state will be made aware of the law in their state, but at the same time they will be offered the option of confidentially working with Project Cuddle and receiving prenatal care as well as other needs that they may have. I am hopeful that many of the other states that are concerned with this issue will follow Colorado's footsteps. It's so exciting to me to know that we can work together with one common goal…saving lives.

You Choose the Ending

Kylie was in terrible pain. She wanted to die. As she gripped the bed sheets the contractions became unbearable. It was almost nine o'clock in the evening and yet both Sandy, her two year old, and Bobby, her one year old, were still up. Kylie knew that she had to feed them and get them to bed. It would be horrible if they saw what was about to happen.

Little Sandy walked from one end of the small, filthy trailer to the other end where Kylie was laying down. "Mama? Mama ouchy?" She was barely old enough to speak, but knew something was wrong with Kylie. She was always a very sensitive little girl. As the contraction subsided, Kylie pulled her body up and headed to the cupboard where she kept the cereal.

"Here sweetie, have some cereal," Kylie offered. She then turned around to find a cardboard medicine box with the name Benadryl on the front. She pulled one pink pill from the box and then placed it in her hand. As she reached for a cup to fill with water, she doubled over with another contraction. Kylie grabbed her belly and leaned against the counter in order to relieve some of the pressure. She moaned as the pain intensified. Finally the contraction passed and she filled the cup.

Just then, little Bobby crawled over to get in on all the action. "Hi buddy," she said as she smiled down at him. "Here, have some Cheerios." She placed a small plastic bowl on the floor that was filled with Bobby's favorite finger food. Kylie then quickly turned her attention toward Sandy. She needed to get her to take this pill so that she would be asleep when things got worse.

It wasn't easy, but Kylie got Sandy to take the pill before she crept back to the bed. She then crushed half of a tablet up and put it in a baby bottle for Bobby. "Here Buba. Drink this." She handed him the bottle and then hoped she could get to the bed before the next contraction. They were now about five minutes apart. Sandy went over to watch the television, even though there wasn't really anything on that would interest a child. She cuddled her little dirty blanket and sucked her thumb as she lay down on the floor and went quietly into a trance. Bobby crawled over to Sandy with his bottle clinched between his teeth. He snuggled next to his big sister. Now, Kylie could take care of everything.

She had no idea what she was going to do. She did not even show. She thought that maybe she wasn't really pregnant. Maybe this was just a really bad period coming on or maybe she was having a miscarriage. After all, she had not missed but a couple of periods. This pain was so bad though. She was afraid to call anyone because she had no medical insurance and if it turned out that she was pregnant she could not afford to have her family find out.

Three hours passed and Sandy was sound asleep with the television now showing an infomercial and Bobby was snuggled up next to her. Neither was in their pajamas, but Kylie did not care. She was now pushing almost constantly. It would not be much longer and still Kylie had no idea what she was going to do when this baby was born. At 3:24a.m. a beautiful little baby slid into the world.

Now it's your turn to choose.

If you want her to call Project Cuddle: go to page 230.

If you think she doesn't call anyone for help read on.

Kylie knew that everyone in her trailer park had just gone to sleep, so she had some time to rest before she cleared her head and figured things out. The baby was a little girl. She had clamped off the umbilical cord with a clothespin before cutting it with a pair of scissors. Though she was breathing on her own, she was very tiny. She did not bother to clean the baby up. Kylie put her in a towel that she found on the bathroom floor.

Kylie had no idea where to go or what to do. She figured that she needed some rest and that she would deal with the baby when she awoke. It was almost seven in the morning when she finally woke up. When Kylie woke up she was very disoriented and was not sure what had happened. When she tried to get up she felt the pain and realized that she had just delivered. She got herself to her feet and then looked over to figure out where she had placed the baby. There on the bed next to her and in a dirty green bath towel lay a small, pink little newborn.

Sandy and Bobby were beginning to rustle in the other room. Kylie had not cleaned up the mess that she had made when giving birth. She had to try and work fast to make this mess disappear. She called her girlfriend, Chloe. Chloe lived two trailers over so she asked if she could watch the children for a few hours. She told Chloe that she had food poisoning and needed to lie down. She hoped that Chloe would take pity on her and watch them all day. Sure enough, it worked. In fact, Chloe offered to let the children spend the night. This was a huge relief to Kylie. Kylie met her at the door with the kids. The baby was back in the bedroom area sleeping, so Chloe did not see her.

By the time Chloe and the children left, Kylie was doubled over in pain. The time had come for her to do something. She went about cleaning the mess from the delivery. She felt as though everything she did was in slow motion. She got a plastic trash bag for the placenta and then threw all the old sheets and bloody towels in with it. She was not about to try and clean those things. It took her many hours to get everything done because she had to stop in between each task. Kylie finished up at around eight o'clock in the evening with everything. The trailer looked better than it had in a long time.

She just didn't know what to do with the baby. Her biggest fear was that if she went to social services they would take her other two children away, or they would contact her family. She couldn't let either of those things happen. She thought about adoption agencies, but knew they would want to talk with the father. That was out of the question. In her mind, he was only a sperm donor. She felt that she had no options.

Kylie put the baby in a banana box that was once used to move things from her former apartment into this trailer. It had gotten a lot of use, and when she put a sheet on the bottom, the baby would be set in there and then a lid put on top. No one would ever know that there was a baby in there. She carried the box out and placed it into the back seat of her old Chevy Nova. The sun was slowly setting now and she was not about to make a move until it was completely dark. She began to drive and everywhere she would go she would either bump into people or discover streetlights. She was hoping to place it somewhere that it could get found right away. She drove by the hospital, but the security guard and cameras at each entrance frightened her away. She thought about the church, but it was Monday morning and most churches were closed on Monday.

Finally, she found the perfect spot. It was a Rescue Mission. People would come in and out almost on an hourly basis seeking shelter. She parked the car back a few buildings from the shelter. She knew that she was in danger of being seen and later pointed out. It took almost twenty minutes before she felt that the coast was clear.

Kylie's heart was pounding so hard. She didn't really feel any attachment to the baby in the box, and in fact was most frightened of being caught. She lifted the box out from the back seat of her car. She could hear the baby squeak as she pulled the box to her chest. Kylie quickly walked to the right side of the main entrance. There was a large container located there that was used as an ashtray. This was the perfect place. Most everyone that came to the shelter smoked, so this was a great place to put it. She set the box down and quickly ran back to her car. Once inside, she looked around one more time to make sure that no one was watching her. Everything was clear. Kylie drove off and felt a huge weight had been taken off her chest. No more baby, no more problems.

222

Kylie arrived home at almost one in the morning. Chloe came out of the neighboring trailer. "Are you okay?" she whispered. "I was worried about you when I saw the car was gone." Kylie was startled. "Oh, I'm alright. I went to the emergency room and they gave me some medicine. Can you keep the kids until the afternoon?" she asked. Chloe reassured her that the children would be fine and then went back into her own trailer.

Kylie collapsed on the bed. She was physically exhausted, but mentally still in high gear. She reached for the remote for the television. She put it on the FOX station. She watched until she dozed off into a deep sleep.

Kylie did not awake until noon on Tuesday. She could feel herself drooling and woke up when she realized what she was doing. As she struggled to sit up, she saw that there was a breaking news story about to come on the station.

If you want the reporter to announce that they found a body: continue below.

If you want the reporter to announce that they found a newborn baby: go to page 228.

The news anchor announced that the body of a baby girl had just been found next to the local rescue mission. "The lifeless body was probably set there during the night." Unfortunately, the baby appears to have been alive at one point and then died from hypothermia." We will bring you new details as they become available to us," said the news anchor.

Kylie's shock grew to fear. Would she get caught? What had gone wrong? These were questions that she would have to live with. Kylie was not feeling very well that following morning. She had stomach pains that were similar to when she was giving birth. She felt as though she was running a fever, but she was too tired to even try to find a thermometer. Her mother had come over that afternoon with a pot of homemade chicken soup and rice pudding. These were two of Kylie's favorites when she was sick. Kylie's mother knocked on the door and waited for Kylie to answer it. She could barely hear a voice faintly in the background telling her to come in. When she got back to where Kylie was lying, she immediately got concerned. "Oh my gosh...you look terrible!" her mother stated. "What's wrong with you?"

Kylie realized that she must look pretty bad, and struggled to try and act more perky so her mother would not be so suspicious and keep asking questions. "I'm fine Ma, I just have really bad cramps. I'll be fine in a couple of hours." Kylie's mother leaned over to readjust the bedding. "It looks like you must have been tossing and turning all night long," she stated as she lifted the sheets to place them at the corner. When she did so, she saw a pool of blood. "Oh my God! You're hemorrhaging!" Kylie was beginning to fade in and out of a conscious state. "I'm okay Ma. It will be fine."

Kylie's mother knew better than that. Kylie was turning a dusky light gray color and was cold to the touch. She knew she had better call 9-1-1 immediately or she could lose her daughter. As she waited for the paramedics, she stood out in front of the old grungy trailer. She waved her arms in the air as they pulled up with the sirens blaring.

"She's inside. I don't know what is causing all the bleeding, but there's a lot! You'd better hurry." The paramedics quickly grabbed their medical cases and ran into the trailer. They bumped the walls with their bodies and then the cases as they struggled to get to the back where Kylie was lying.

They began to take her vitals and then looked at each other. They knew that she was in bad shape. They never said a word to each other about their suspicions, but they called for a helicopter ambulance. Kylie's blood pressure was dangerously low and her color was very bad. They needed to get her to a hospital in the next twenty minutes or she would die.

They started IV's and prepared Kylie for transporting. They did not have enough space to try and work with a backboard, so they decided to carefully carry her out as soon as they heard the helicopter approaching.

The vibrations of the helicopter could be felt as it approached. Outside, the police had cleared off an area and blocked traffic so that the helicopter could land. It set down in the empty field next to the trailer park. Once it set down, the nurse on board jumped out of the helicopter and ran towards Kylie's trailer. Once he acquainted himself with the case, the paramedics helped get Kylie out of the trailer and onto the backboard that was leaning up against the trailer.

Once she was strapped on, they quickly got her onboard the Life Flight Helicopter. This was her only hope for survival. Kylie's mother was instructed to drive to the hospital. She was too nervous to drive and asked a neighbor if she would be willing to take her there. She arrived almost twenty minutes after Kylie arrived. The social worker greeted her at the entrance and began to ask questions. Some of the questions seemed unusual and others seemed stupid.

Kylie was completely unconscious when she finally got to the hospital. The trauma team began to work on her immediately. It did not take them long to figure out that Kylie had given birth within the past two days. She had not delivered the entire placenta after giving birth. She had developed peritonitis and was now fighting for her life. The police had been called in. They felt certain that the baby girl who had been found dead that morning had been born to Kylie.

The police brought in some of their top investigators. They took samples of blood, urine and just about everything else they could get their hands on. Within an hour they had a search warrant for Kylie's trailer and had roped it completely off. Kylie was moved to the Intensive Care Unit and had not regained consciousness.

Kylie's mother sat in the ICU waiting room for what seemed like hours. An officer approached her. She could not figure out why the police would be interested in this situation. It was obvious to her that this was a "personal, female problem" and it was none of their concern. The officer sat down next to her and explained that the doctors had found the placenta of a full term baby within Kylie's uterus. The officer asked if she had any idea where Kylie might have taken the baby.

The poor woman was in complete shock. She could not accept what the officer was saying. After all, Kylie was a great mother to her two children. She and Kylie had a very good relationship. There is no way that her daughter could have given birth. After all, she had seen her daughter every day and she did not even look pregnant.

The doctor came out to meet with Kylie's mother and the officer, "Kylie's hanging in there. The next twenty-four hours are the most critical. She lost a lot of blood." The officer wanted to know when he might be able to interview Kylie. He was not happy when the doctor told him it could be a couple of days and blurted out, "What if she left that baby out somewhere and it's still alive. We need to speak with her as soon as possible." Though the doctor wanted to help, he believed that this was not going to be possible for quite some time.

The days that followed were extremely tough on Kylie's mother. She wanted so much to be able to believe in her daughter. The children had been placed into foster care and hopefully would be released to Kylie's mother. The courts would not guarantee that placement, but it was the only hope that they had of staying in the family.

Kylie was moved out of ICU after four days. The police had found enough evidence to place her under arrest. She had an officer stationed outside her hospital room door 24 hours a day. She admitted to the detectives what had happened two days after being moved out of ICU. She knew that there was major evidence staked against her and she would be doing herself a favor if she let them know what she had done. She told them that she had no intention of letting the baby die. She was sure that with as many people that went past the mission there would be someone picking it up within minutes of being dropped off.

For the next three years Kylie spent her life behind bars. Sandy and Bobby had been placed in relative foster care with Kylie's mother. She has since adopted the children. Kylie will be getting out of prison in one more year and will be on probation for three more years.

Sandy and Bobby have not seen their mother since she was taken away. They are not aware of what went on that fateful night and Kylie has not figured out how or if she will tell them.

The state ended up paying for legal fees, foster care expenses, and the cost of keeping Kylie in prison. The expenses would have been much higher if Kylie had not pled guilty. That would have added the expenses of a complete trial.

The End

If you want the reporter to announce that they found a newborn baby.

The news reporter was announcing that a very pale newborn baby girl was found in a box outside the local rescue mission. She was rushed to the Children's Hospital and was listed in serious condition. Kylie was scared that she would be found out, but was relieved to hear that the baby was alive.

Kylie's shock grew to fear. Would she get caught? What had gone wrong? These were questions that she would have to live with. Kylie was not feeling very well that following morning. She had stomach pains that were similar to when she was giving birth. She felt as though she were running a fever, but was too tired to even try to find a thermometer. Her mother had come over that afternoon with a pot of homemade chicken soup and rice pudding. These were two of Kylie's favorites when she was sick. Kylie's mother knocked on the door and waited for Kylie to answer it. She could barely hear a voice faintly in the background telling her to come in. When she got back to where Kylie was lying, she immediately got concerned. "Oh my gosh…you look terrible!" her mother stated. "What's wrong with you?"

Kylie realized that she must look pretty bad, and struggled to try and act more perky so her mother would not be so suspicious and keep asking questions. "I'm fine Ma, I just have really bad cramps. I'll be fine in a couple of hours." Kylie's mother leaned over to readjust the bedding, "It looks like you must have been tossing and turning all night long." "I'll be fine in a couple of days. Can you take the kids for me, Ma?" Her mother agreed to take the two little ones and after serving up a bowl of rice pudding for Kylie, she gathered up some diapers and clothes and then left.

Kylie followed the news for the next few days. She heard that the baby was doing better. The doctors had given her the name of "Baby Grace" because they felt that if she had been found just ten minutes later, she would have died. It was God's grace that saved her. Baby Grace would now go into foster care where she would remain while the detectives continued to investigate. They had to

228

allow time for the parents to either come forward or get caught.

Kylie had been very clever. She had left no evidence behind. For the past three years Kylie has lived looking over her shoulder. She still has nightmares about the child she dropped off like yesterday's trash. She hopes that this is a secret she can take to her grave.

Though expenses were limited for an investigation, medical help and foster care for Baby Grace, the holes in Baby Grace's life as well as Kylie's are permanent. Kylie will never know where Grace ended up and Baby Grace will never know of her medical history, or family tree. Perhaps the biggest hole that will be in Baby Grace's heart is that of not knowing why she was dumped off like a bad batch of bananas.

The End

If you choose for Kylie to call Project Cuddle...

Kylie quickly wrapped the baby in a pillowcase from the pillow that was once placed under her head. She was so glad that the children were still sound asleep. This gave her some time to figure things out. She knew that she was going to have to keep her Mama away from the trailer. The last time Kylie was pregnant, Mama went ballistic. After Bobby was born, Mama would not even come near Kylie or the kids for the next six months. It took Mama's brother dying to finally unify the two. It had been his dying wish that they get back together. Mama held up her end of the bargain and shortly before he died, they got back together.

Kylie passed out shortly after giving birth. She came to just after the sun rose. She picked up a small piece of paper that had been left there over six months earlier by a friend who was pregnant. She dialed the toll-free number and heard the woman on the other end of the line. She couldn't bring herself to say anything. As frightened as she was of having Mama discover this baby, she was even more frightened of the voice at the other end of the phone. She quickly hung up.

For the next two weeks Kylie hid this tiny little girl in the closet of her trailer. She had clamped off the umbilical cord with a wooden clothespin and cleaned it off with alcohol each day. It was a small baby, about five pounds, so she slept most of the time. Kylie still had powdered formula that she used for Bobby, so she would just make up a bit of that once in awhile for the baby.

Finally, after two very long weeks Kylie realized that she had to do something. She was exhausted. She was healing well, but was not getting enough sleep. She was nervous because she was so afraid that someone would find out the truth. She ended up picking up the phone and dialing Project Cuddle's number again. This time she knew she had to stay on the line. If she didn't, she was afraid of what her next move would be.

I answered the phone and reassured Kylie that we could help. I could tell that she was not at all attached to the baby. She begged

230

me to find her a volunteer. She was not able to keep this baby and needed someone to come over and give her a break immediately. I was finally able to convince her to give me a phone number. I promised to call her back with a volunteer's phone number.

I called a volunteer by the name of Shelly Roberts. She had helped us out on a case a few months earlier and was at work when I called this time. Shelly was ready to take a ride down to assess the situation. I called Kylie to let her know that Shelly would be coming to see her. No one was going to force her into anything, but we wanted her to know that help was on the way.

Three hours after that call came in, Shelly was at Kylie's front door. Shelly didn't know quite what to expect. As the trailer door opened Shelly saw a disheveled looking woman in her early twenties. "Hello, are you Shelly?" Kylie asked as she lowered her head. She was too uncomfortable to make eye contact with Shelly.

Shelly was invited into the trailer where she saw and heard no signs of a baby. Both Sandy and Bobby were busy playing with blocks on the floor. Little Sandy would stack them and then Bobby would swing his arms and make them fall back down. He would giggle each time that they hit the ground. Sandy would exclaim, "Oh Bobby!" Then she would smile and giggle. Shelly was afraid to bring up the subject of the baby. The two women sat down at the little laminated tabletop that served as a dining room table and doubled as a fold down bed at night. Kylie broke down when she began to talk with Shelly. She could barely stand the baby and needed to get rid of it before her family figured it out. Finally, Shelly learned that the baby was still alive.

Shelly reached her hand across the table and on top of Kylie's hand. She felt that she could now safely ask where the baby was. She was fearful of upsetting Kylie, but knew that this had to be done soon. Kylie told Shelly that she would take her to the baby. They rose from their seats and headed toward the back of the trailer. Shelly was not sure what she should be preparing for, but decided she would be able to handle whatever came her way.

Kylie opened the closet door, and there on the floor on top of a bunch of old blankets was the baby. She was so tiny that she did not look real. Shelly asked Kylie if it would be all right if she picked up the baby. "Whatever you want," Kylie said. "Just close the door. I don't want the kids to see it." Shelly picked up the baby and held it to her breast. She looked over at Kylie to make sure that she was not upset by this action. Kylie looked straight into Shelly's eyes and asked, "Do you mind if I smoke?" The last thing that Shelly wanted to do was to upset Kylie, so she said, "No problem." As Shelly held the baby, she could tell that the baby had been taken care of, but would definitely be better off if she was in a home where she was being nurtured.

Shelly felt as though Kylie was more comfortable now and so she felt brave enough to ask a few questions. The first thing she asked Kylie was if the baby had been easy to care for? Kylie told her that the baby had not been any problem at all. Then she ventured on to another question that she was a little apprehensive in asking. "Have you named the baby?" Kylie got a serious look on her face. "Since I don't want her I didn't think about naming her. Every day I thought I would get up the courage to call you guys, but I would chicken out at the last minute. I had no idea she would be here so long. I'm sorry." Kylie began to apologize to Shelly. Shelly knew that she needed to get her out of this mode and so she began to talk to her about the different options that lay before her. It wasn't long and Kylie's tone was better.

I waited anxiously for the phone call telling me that the baby was safe. It seemed as though it took forever. It was almost five hours after Shelly arrived and we finally got the call. "Hey Debbe, it's me...Shelly. I'm here with Kylie and it looks like she wants to find a family for her baby." I asked to speak with Kylie.

The conversation went very well. We talked about her future and the baby's, as well as the other children. It was definitely going to be best for her to find parents for this child. No one would ever know that she had even been pregnant.

Shelly took the little baby home for the night and allowed Kylie a bit of time to rethink everything. If this was what she really wanted, we would search until the family she wanted was found.

There was a precious little couple by the name of Debra and James Hartley in a neighboring town. They had two grown daughters and loved children dearly. They had toyed with the idea of adopting, but the time just had not been right. Now, with their backgrounds and the particular wishes of Kylie, it looked to be the perfect time for them to consider adopting.

Within a matter of days, the Hartley's had begun adoption proceedings and had this little angel in their arms. They named her Nikki. Someday she would know of her past and how much she was wanted.

✧✧ UPDATE ✧✧

Today little Miss Nikki, rescue baby #174, is known all across town. Everyone in town dotes on her and feels honored to have her as one of their own. The Hartleys stay in touch with us and cannot imagine their world without Nikki. They are forever grateful to Kylie for allowing them the privilege of adopting and raising her daughter. Kylie is doing well with the two children she is raising. She is a good mother to them and her family never found out about little Nikki. She has chosen not to stay in touch with the Hartley Family.

THIS WAS THE REAL ENDING. OH, BY THE WAY…
THEY LIVED HAPPILY EVER AFTER.

My Dream Has Come True!

Saturday, August 7, 2001

I was on my way down to Sharon Plumb's home in Aliso Viejo. She had put together a neighborhood block party complete with a little train for the children to ride on and loads of food. I brought Jonathon and Tyler on the twenty-minute ride. They were excited about all the fun they were about to have.

Just as I pulled into the parking area, I got a call from my daughter-in-law Talea. A call had come in from a woman on the crisis line. This woman, Patricia, needed immediate help. The good news was that she was within forty minutes of my current location. She did not want her baby and decided that she wanted us to meet her at a local school where she would hand it over to us. She told Talea that she didn't even have a diaper or blanket for the baby. She was not at all prepared for this.

Needless to say, both boys missed out on their train ride that afternoon, but it was worth it. I quickly got Patricia's phone number and turned the Cuddle Van around to head toward home where I would drop off the boys and pick up Talea. But, when I tried to call Patricia, she would not answer the phone. I called Talea back and asked her to call while I headed towards home. Maybe Patricia had caller I.D. and would only pick up if she knew it was the number Talea had spoken to her on before.

234

I quickly made a call to a local volunteer to locate formula, diapers, blankets and clothes while I continued driving the last ten miles back home. As I rounded the last turn, I saw the drop off of baby items taking place. Perfect timing. Jonathon got out of the van as Talea got in. I wanted a co-pilot on this mission since there was no time for mistakes. Tyler wanted to come along since he loved adventure and babies. Our main nurturer, Emily was ready to come along as well. This whole thing was moving like clockwork. We did not skip a beat.

On our way up, Talea spoke with Patricia a little more in depth. She found out that Patricia had just delivered at home and as Talea listened to the baby screaming in the background, discovered that there was nothing there for the baby. Patricia was extremely anxious for us to get to the field where we were to meet. We were just as anxious. She gave us the last portion of the instructions on how to get there and then hung up so that she could get herself ready. As we were getting closer she would be wrapping the baby in a towel and then placing it in a tote bag in order to smuggle it out of her apartment complex. Patricia told us that she believed that the baby was in no immediate danger, and would be fine until we got to her. When we again brought up the idea of her calling 9-1-1, she again refused.

Everyone in the van was anxious to get to the selected drop-off. As I made a left at the last street before our destination, I was able to spot the bleachers that Patricia had spoken of. Angel always drives the unmarked vehicle, but had been sick that day, so we had to show up in the Cuddle Van with words displayed on both side and the back that read, "Don't Abandon Your Baby...call Project Cuddle". The last thing I wanted to do was spook her with the van, so I dropped off Talea and Emily at the corner just before the bleachers. I would drive past them and wait at the far end. Both Emily and Talea thought they saw the woman sitting on the bleachers and so they grabbed the blanket and shut the doors to the van. I rolled down the passenger window and told them to take a cell phone with them just in case a problem arose.

I drove past the bleachers, but realized that the woman they were headed towards was not the woman they were to meet. Then, about two sets of bleachers down, I saw a woman slouched over on the first row that I was pretty certain was Patricia. I quickly called Talea and said, "I found her, go past the bleachers and head towards me." Emily and Talea, in her third trimester of pregnancy, ran towards the woman. I made a u-turn and actually passed Patricia and parked several hundred yards in front of the bleachers she was sitting on. Now, I would have to wait for the pass-off.

I had butterflies in my stomach as I watched everything that was going on through the side mirror. Everything went just as planned. We got Patricia to sign the paper for emergency medical treatment and then Emily took the baby that was still in the dirty, old, rust colored towel. Emily wrapped a new, thermal blanket around the towel that held the baby and then carefully walked the precious package towards me. Emily had handled many, many babies over the years, but I had never seen her carry one quite like this. Emily later told me that she was so afraid of dropping the baby and so she had walked extra slow and cautious. When Emily reached the van, she started to get into the back seat, but I told her she needed to bring the baby to the front seat so I could evaluate the situation. If she were not stable then I would drive around the corner and call 9-1-1. We could either stay at one specific spot and wait for the ambulance, or head towards Garden Grove Community Hospital and meet the ambulance part way.

The baby looked good, but her feet were blue and I knew that we needed to get her body temperature up as soon as possible. The smell of the dirty, unbathed newborn was not a pleasant smell at all. She smelled of old blood, afterbirth and who knows what. She had large areas of her scalp that were crusted over with blood and other foreign matter, but still I could tell that this was a beautiful little baby underneath. Tyler had pulled out the "Emergency Delivery Kit" that we carried in the Cuddle Van just in case we needed to use it. I told him to look for the umbilical clamp in case it was necessary. It was a miracle! I looked at the belly button and discovered that it was not clamped off or tied off. It had been cut so extremely close to the baby's belly that there was no place to even put a clamp. All I could figure was that somehow, it had miracu-

236

lously sealed itself off while she was wrapped up in the towel. It looked nasty, with little bumps all over a bloody stub, but it would be fine for now, so Tyler put the kit away.

I looked back to see where Talea was and why she had not come back to the vehicle. Talea and Patricia had been standing near the bleachers and I realized that they were now both heading towards the van. Talea was motioning for me to back up the van so that Patricia did not have to walk so far. I started the heater up inside the van even though the temperature was 75 degrees. I then instructed Emily to get into the back of the van with the baby and keep her wrapped up tightly and hold her close to add her own body heat. Emily quickly got to the back seat and then handed the tiny bundle to Tyler while she fastened her seat belt.

As the van got closer to Patricia, Talea opened up the front passenger's door. Patricia got in and collapsed into the front seat. "I'm so dizzy," she said. Talea told me that Patricia wanted a ride back to her apartment. I asked Patricia if she had delivered the placenta and she told me that she was not sure. I told her that I was worried about her and thought that it would be a really good idea if we took both she and the baby to the hospital to be examined. I explained that no one would have to know. It was our secret.

The smell of fresh blood, old blood, and afterbirth was strong. We needed the car to be warm for the baby but we were all extremely sensitive to the combination of odors that were awakening our senses. We cheated, and put the heater on low and the windows down just a bit to get fresh air. It only took a minute for Patricia to tell me that she was willing to go to the hospital, with the understanding that it was all to be done very confidentially. No one from her family could ever know about this. I instructed Talea to call one of the obstetricians we often used and let him know about the situation, while I used the other cell phone to contact the emergency room and let them know that we were on the way.

On the way to the hospital I discovered how the baby's umbilical cord had stopped bleeding. Patricia explained to us that she had delivered the baby and then set her down on the bathroom floor.

She began cleaning up the mess that had been made during the delivery and began stacking the dirty towels on the floor. Once she made a fair amount of progress, she took a shower. It wasn't until she stepped out of the shower that she heard the distant cry of a baby. She realized that the baby was under the stack of towels and began to search for her. All we can figure is that the weight of the towels was enough to stop the bleeding of the umbilical cord, yet there was enough air that she was able to breathe.

As I got to the emergency room entrance, I asked the male nurse that was standing just outside the ambulance entrance if I should park there to drop off the baby and Patricia. He told me this was fine. He went in to get a wheelchair while I lifted the baby out of Emily's arms and headed toward the double doors.

The nurses were all busy with other patients when I walked in. I went to the reception desk with the baby wrapped in a towel and quickly got the attention of the receptionist. "Oh, we heard you were bringing in the mother, but didn't know anything about the baby," she stated. "I did not realize that I needed to mention that both were coming in, I just assumed..."

They quickly put me into a room and had a triage nurse come over to evaluate the baby that now slept in my arms. For the first time I really got a good look at her. Her skin was beautiful porcelain white. Her cheeks had just the right amount of pink. Each moment that I looked at her made me fall that much more in love with her. She was precious. She passed each test they gave her with flying colors. It was only when they saw her umbilical cord that they became alarmed. It was a large dried up, red piece of flesh. "We'll have to treat this," the nurse said as she looked up at me and spoke. "She is one lucky baby. She could have bled to death or died of sepsis if you had not brought her in." I knew she was right and so glad that Patricia had called.

Both mother and baby were settled in by 7:30 p.m. It had only been three hours since Patricia had given birth, but she was doing very well, and the baby was now in NICU with IV antibiotics. The baby would remain on antibiotics over the next seven days and she

238

would then be able to leave the hospital. My heart reeled with all kinds of different emotions during this whole event. I found myself unable to think of anything but this beautiful little baby. Though we have saved over three hundred and fifty babies in the past five years, I believe this is the baby that I longed to save for the past 37 years. She will always hold a piece of my heart and I will pray for her safety and well-being for the rest of my life. She magically touched so many lives in just a very short time. Some families have decided to "Rescue" babies because they have seen her and others have chosen to volunteer. Dave and I actually considered adopting her and many tears were shed, but as tough as it was for us to decide not to adopt, we both feel that it will be best for Hope to move onto another family. This way I can continue my efforts to save more little miracles through Project Cuddle.

✧✧ UPDATE ✧✧

Patricia realized that she did not want this baby, but wanted to be a part of finding her daughter a new home. She has found new friendship in her volunteer Kathleen McArdle. Kathleen has been instrumental in helping Patricia deal with each aspect of her situation. Patricia met with several families and then chose the perfect one for her needs. She named her daughter Hope and let me pick the middle name...Rose. I was fortunate to be able to hold and feed Hope Rose, rescue baby #347, for a few weeks. I, like my children, fell in love with her and am happy to say that I got to watch as Patricia handed Hope over to her new adoptive mother. After placing her into Stacey's arms, Patricia said, "Now this is your new mommy. She's going to take care of you." We all had tears in our eyes as we watched Patricia walk away with dignity and pride. What began as a tragic situation ended in a beautiful and touching way.

Footnotes

1 Kathy Cribari Hamer, "Save the lives of abandoned babies," North Texas Catholic , August 20, 1999, p.20

2 Esther Haynes, "STRANGER THAN FICTION," JANE, April 2000, p.95

3 S. K. Bardwell, "Abandoned baby safe/Sisters find 11-pound newborn at complex," Houston Chronicle, April 19, 2000, p. 21 Metfront

4 Deanna Boyd, "A Gift of God," Star-Telegram, January 26, 2000, p.13A

5 Nina Bernstein, "Few Women Choose to Abandon Newborns at Legal Havens," The New York Times, August 31, 2001

Photo Credits

GET IN TOUCH WITH
Project Cuddle

Project Cuddle
2973 Harbor Blvd., #326
Costa Mesa, CA 92626

To volunteer or donate
714-432-9681

If you are pregnant and need help
1-888-628-3353

Web Site: www.projectcuddle.org
Email: cuddle1@ix.netcom.com
Fax: 714-433-6815

How Can You Help Save A Baby?

The best news of all is that people are trying to stop this tragedy. You too can make a difference. Whether it's time, talent or money...all are needed to continue our efforts. To be honest, the sky is the limit. Here are just a few examples of people who have made a difference in the lives of many.

Julie Culp received $100 from the pastor of her church. She was told to take that money and make it multiply. The fruits of her efforts really paid off. She paid for all the invitations, food and decorations for a baby shower for one of our girls who had absolutely no family support. The girl was in a car accident and while having tests run the doctor discovered that she was pregnant. Upon closer examination they found that she was around seven months along. A month before Sandy's due date, we were able to get her everything she and the baby could possibly need for the months to come, as well as support and a labor coach. Her baby was born safely and was healthy. She walked away with piece of mind, knowing that she did the right thing, and knowing that people really do care about her and her baby.

Actresses Jill Whelan from "The Love Boat" and Crystal Martell created their own designer line of jewelry. A portion of the profits go directly to Project Cuddle.

A long time supporter of Project Cuddle unfortunately passed away and made her last donation to us through her will. She once sent me a hand painted plate that had a picture of an angel looking over a baby. It hangs over our fireplace to this day and will continue to in remembrance of her.

Some Sunday school groups have held car washes and bake sales while others have done garage sales. If every church donated $5 each month, we would be able to reach so many precious lives. Perhaps you can educate your synagogue, congregation or club. Project Cuddle has come such a long way in the first six years, saving over 436 babies as well as their mothers. It is only through the help of you and those in your community that we will be able to continue this uphill climb. I am hoping that because of the stories inside this book you are now looking to see how you as an individual can make a difference in the life of the tiniest victim...a baby.